icons

LEARNING RESOURCES CENTRE
John Paul II School

Mary Jo Martin, RSHM

Anne White

Ann Brook

Paul Gray

Yvonne May

Damian Walmsley

with

Tony Castle

Simon Danes

Jane Ranzetta

LIVING
Catholic Bishops' Conference
of England & Wales
Sharing
a national project
of catechesis &
religious education
OUR FAITH

Collins

Published by HarperCollins*Publishers* Ltd
77–85 Fulham Palace Road
London W6 8JB

© Department for Catholic Education and Formation, Bishops' Conference of
England and Wales

www.**Collins**Educational.com
On-line support for schools and colleges

First published 2000

Reprinted 2000, 2001

ISBN 0 00 322130 X

Nihil Obstat Fr Anton Cowan, *censor*

Imprimatur Mgr Thomas Egan, V.G.
Westminster, 29th June 2000

The Nihil obstat and Imprimatur are a declaration that a book or pamphlet is considered to
be free from doctrinal or moral error. It is not implied that those who have granted the Nihil
obstat and imprimatur agree with the contents, opinions or statements expressed.

British Library Cataloguing in Publication Data
A catalogue record for this book is available from the British Library

Project management by Terry Vittachi

Picture research by Kathy Lockley

Design and layout by Ken Vail Graphic Design, Cambridge

Cover design by Ken Vail Graphic Design, Cambridge

Cover photograph
1 Christie's Images Ltd 2000
2 The Telegraph Colour Library
3 Tony Stone Images
4 Tony Stone Images

Printed and bound by Scotprint

Illustrations
David Eaton, pp. 36, 56, 77; Rosamund Fowler, pp. 28, 37, 57, 64, 69, 74, 76, 78, 81, 82, 91,
92, 95, 96; Paul McCaffrey, pp. 9, 18, 23, 41, 42, 43, 54, 55, 59, 66, 87; Curtis Tappenden,
pp. 6, 29, 35, 53, 58, 67, 68, 75, 84.

Photographs
AA Photolibrary p.47; AKG London/BL pp.17, 19, 21, 33, 39, 63, 72, 73, 80; Andes Press
Agency pp.10, 12, 33, 52, 65, 71; *L'Arche* p.26; Art Directors & TRIP Photo Library pp.30, 31,
32, 45, 49, 65, 71, 72, 89, 90, 93, 94; Bridgeman Art Library London & New York p.19;
CAFOD pp.27, 45; CIRCA Photo Library pp.33, 48, 49, 50, 51; Robert Harding Picture
Library pp.20, 41, 47, 65, 79, 80, 88; Philomena McDermott, Heronbrook p.86; Natural
Bridges p.26; The News Studio p.26; PA Photos pp.15, 40; St Paul Multimedia Productions
UK p.42; Anthony Reynolds Gallery, London p.19; Rex Features p.85; Tony Stone Images
pp.7, 34; *Vie de Jesus Mafa*, Versailles p.63; John Walmsley Photo Library pp. 7, 16, 22

Text
Excerpts from the English translation of Rite of Baptism for Children © 1969, International
Committee on English in the Liturgy, Inc. (ICEL); excerpts from the English translation of Rite
of Holy Week © 1972, ICEL; excerpts from the English translation of The Roman Missal ©
1973, ICEL; excerpts from the English translation of Rite of Penance © 1974, ICEL; excerpts
from the English translation of Dedication of a Church and Altar © 1978, ICEL.
All rights reserved.

Foreword

On behalf of the Bishops' Conference, I am very pleased to welcome the publication of *Icons*.

Diocesan RE advisers, teachers and many others from all the dioceses of England and Wales have worked extremely hard in the production of this programme, which forms an important part of the National Project. I thank them for their dedication and perseverance.

At the Low Week 2000 Meeting of the Bishops' Conference of England and Wales, the bishops published a statement on Religious Education in Catholic Schools. In it they said that the primary purpose of classroom religious education in a Catholic school is:

'To draw pupils into a systematic study of the teaching of the Church, the saving mystery of Christ which the Church proclaims.' (para 7)

In undertaking this task, schools will benefit greatly from the provision of good teaching resources. For this reason I welcome *Icons*, for it will help Catholic schools to fulfil these expectations during the critical years of Key Stage Three.

In their statement, the bishops also stated:

'The importance of the teacher of RE cannot be exaggerated. We are most grateful to all those teachers who, week in and week out, have contributed to the religious education of pupils in our schools … We salute the generosity of the teachers who have brought not only a love of their faith to their teaching but also a deep concern for the well-being of every pupil.' (para 12)

I gladly repeat that thanks and express my own encouragement for teachers in their important task.

Archbishop Vincent Nichols
Chairman
Department for Catholic Education and Formation

6 June 2000

Acknowledgements

Icons is the fruit of a shared vision, commitment and work. It derives its strength from a long and rigorous process of consultation with Bishops, Diocesan RE advisers, teachers and students of all twenty-two dioceses of England and Wales. It is a key component of the Bishops' national project of catechesis and religious education.

Thanks, first of all, to Bishop Edwin Regan, Chairman of the Steering Committee of the National Project for his leadership and commitment and the members of that Committee: Mr Anthony Clark, Canon Peter Humfrey, Sr Victoria Hummell, Rev Liam Kelly, Mrs Oona Stannard and Rev George Stokes.

Thanks to the Bishops' Conference and in particular to Archbishops Patrick Kelly and Vincent Nichols, Bishops Daniel Mullins, Edwin Regan and Peter Smith for their time and attention in the final stages of scrutiny.

Since 1996, Diocesan secondary RE advisers and teacher representatives have been actively involved in the development of Icons. For their time, energy and expertise thanks to: Rev Joseph Quigley, Miss Collette Dawson, Rev Ieuan Wyn Jones, Rev Dennis Sutton, Miss Marjorie Parker, Rev Sean Hall, Miss Anne Sales, Miss Sheila O'Brien, Mr Nicholas Weeks, Rev Nigel Bavidge, Rev Des Seddon, Mr Tony Lamb, Sr Aidan Richards, Sr Margaret Horan, Ms Anne-Marie McIntosh, Sr Maura McMenamin, Mr Adrian Dempsey, Mrs Rita Price, Br Charles Gay, Mr Paul Uden, Mr Paul Rowland, Rev Adrian Morrin, and Ms Noreen O'Neill, secondary advisor of CAFOD. Thanks also to the teachers and students of the schools in every diocese who took part in the monitored trial in 1999 for their support. We hope they will recognise some of their ideas in the final text.

Particular thanks to those who were involved in early stages of development: Mr Tony Castle, Mrs Jane Ranzetta, Mr Simon Danes and to their families and schools: St Bernard's School Wescliff on Sea, New Hall School, Chelmsford and Cardinal Newman, Hove. Also to Maria Ivko whose creative contribution remains as a lasting memorial to her dedication to Catholic education. May she rest in peace.

Special thanks to Dr Thomas Allain-Chapman, Commissioning Editor at HarperCollins with whom the professional aspects of the work became a sharing of ideas that enhanced the development of Icons.

To Sisters Mary, Elizabeth and Cecelia and the staff at the Kairos Centre for their hospitality, interest and encouragement and care for our well-being during long working sessions.

To our families, and friends we owe tremendous gratitude. They, too, laboured with us through their understanding, patience and listening. Special thanks to Sr Mary Jo's community of the Religious of the Sacred Heart of Mary, and colleagues at St Mary's College, Strawberry Hill, to Anne's colleagues at the Catholic Education Service and to the headteachers, staff and students of St Angela's, Forest Gate, St Bede's, Scunthorpe, St Benedict's Whitehaven, St Bonaventure's, Forest Gate and St Mary's College, Hull. We could not have completed the task without your support.

Finally, thanks to all those involved in the final stages of production: text editor, picture research, designers, artists and photographers.

The journey has been long. In one sense, with the publication of the text, it has just begun. It has been a tremendous privilege to be part of the creation and development of Icons. Our hope is that teachers and students will find here a programme of religious education that enables, illumines and leads to a discovery of the power of faith and the adventure that is the search for meaning and for God.

Mary Jo Martin RSHM, Anne White, Ann Brook, Paul Gray, Yvonne May, Damian Walmsley

To my community of the Religious of the Sacred Heart of Mary, a special thank you, for continued support, encouragement and most of all, for listening; and to George Stokes – a priest, teacher and friend – to whom my work is dedicated.

Contents

1A About belonging

Check out what you know ☑

In groups of four, on large sheets of paper, do a spider graph of the word 'Community' and another of the word 'Church'.

Think and talk

1. Name some groups and communities you belong to.
2. Belonging means…
   With a partner, list five advantages and five disadvantages of belonging.
3. With a partner, improvise or write a dialogue in which one person is *for* belonging and the other is *against*. Include as many ideas from your lists as you can.

Work as a class

1 ◆ Match the different meanings in 'Words we use' with your lists of groups and communities.
2 ◆ How is a school a community?
3 ◆ How many different groups make up the school community?
4 ◆ Display your findings.

In this section of our work we will be learning:

◆ what it means to belong to different kinds of groups and communities
◆ that the Church is the community of believers called by God.

Words we use

'group'

▶ people standing together
▶ people working together for as long as it takes to do one task
▶ people classed together, such as tall, red-haired, car drivers
▶ people coming together to share an interest, such as a fan club

'community'

▶ people who share something in common, such as a way of life, nationality
▶ people who share religious belief, such as a community of faith
▶ people who live together and follow a common way of life, such as a religious community
▶ people who agree to share their resources, such as the European Union

Thought stop

Imagine… your ideal community.

Do you speak the language?

Work as a class

1 ◆ Brainstorm words that belong to the following
   groups: maths, art, geography, football or
   another sport, music, ICT, space travel.
2 ◆ Which words belong to more than one group?
3 ◆ Which words change their meanings from one
   group to another?

A family, a group of friends and a school can have their
own language. Knowing this can make the difference
between belonging and not belonging, being 'in' or 'out'.

1. Look back to your work on belonging. Do your groups or
   communities have a special language of belonging?
2. Think of two or three examples of language that you know
   and use because you belong to a group or community.
3. Record your ideas. Write a short paragraph or poem,
   draw a cartoon or use your ICT skills.
4. Write one sentence to explain how you would feel if you
   were in a group and did not know the language.

Let's find out about the community called the Church

What makes a church?

Work in groups: half take *Recipe 1* and the others *Recipe 2*.

1. Read the list of ingredients carefully.
2. Talk about what you would end up with if you followed this recipe.
3. Would you need any other ingredients to make a church?

Recipe 1

You will need:

10 tons of cement

50,000 bricks

2 tons of plaster

300 feet of planking

500 feet of electrical cable

50 light fittings

40 panes of glass

1 large sheet of marble

Recipe 2

You will need:

lots of different people of

- all ages from babies to 90+

- both sexes

- different nationalities

- different races

- different backgrounds

- lots of different gifts

- lots of different skills

Work as a class

1 ◆ What will you make if you follow *Recipe 1*?
2 ◆ What will you make if you follow *Recipe 2*?
3 ◆ Which way of building a church will take longer?

Extra!

◆ Write out the instructions for *Recipe 2*.

People first

It is likely that there is a building called a church in your neighbourhood.
When the Christian Church began it was very different.

A *People **heard** the good news of Jesus.*

The Church is the people God gathers in the whole world.

B *They **gathered** for the breaking of the bread.*

C *They **lived in a new way** in the spirit of Jesus. They shared whatever they had.*

The gatherings of believers were called 'ekklesia', a Greek word meaning 'called out'. St Paul's letters begin with greetings to the 'ekklesia'. When Christianity became the official religion of the Roman Empire, Christians had their own buildings. These were called 'ecclesia' or 'domus Domini', Latin for 'the Lord's House'.

Today, 'church' is used to mean both the building where people gather to worship and the community who follow and share the good news of Jesus.

Words we use

The Greek word for 'the Lord's [house]' is *kyriakon*. From it come:

English	*church*	Welsh	*eglwys* (say *eggloys*)
Scots	*kirk*	French	*église*
German	*kirche*	Irish	*teach an phobal* (say *teeok un foble*)
Dutch	*kerk*		– the house of the people

1A About belonging

The local Church

Look carefully at the words and pictures below.

Talk about what they tell you about:

1. the different people who belong to a parish community
2. different ways of belonging
3. what they get from belonging
4. how they contribute to the life of the parish
5. how they feel about belonging.

Hello! I'm Jill Fisher. I help with Children's Liturgy of the Word at the 10 o'clock Mass every Sunday.

I've been coming to St Mark's for two months. I'm new in the neighbourhood. I think I'd like to join the Justice and Peace group because I'm interested in CAFOD's work in Third World countries.

We're making posters for a sponsored walk. It's to raise money for HCPT. The Youth Group do this every year. Last time we got enough for two people to go to Lourdes.

I'm in the music group. We play at the 11.30 Mass twice a month.

I'm Father Peter. I've been parish priest at St Mark's for seven years.

I've been part of the SVP group at St Mark's for two years. It all started when Jim Fernandez asked if I could spare an hour to help him to drop off a table and chairs to one of the families the SVP were helping.

I was baptised at St Mark's but I don't belong to anything. I don't go to Mass very often, but I like to go at Christmas.

We were married in St Mark's and next week we are going to celebrate our Golden Wedding anniversary. We're having a special Mass and a get-together for all the family in the parish hall.

I'm Mary McWilliams. I can't get out any more. Joyce Kelly brings me Holy Communion every Sunday. She's a special minister of Holy Communion. But I miss going to church.

Read more about St Mark's in *Copymaster* [2]

Make a record of your work

1. Write down three new things you have learned about a parish community.
2. Name three different ways of belonging.
3. What does a special minister of Holy Communion do?
4. What do you think the parish could do to welcome newcomers?
5. What do you think the parish could do to keep in touch with people who only come to church at Christmas?
6. What do you think the SVP group is for?
7. If you belonged to this parish, which group would you join? Why?

The diocese

Parishes belong to a diocese. Each diocese has a bishop. He is the leader of the local Church. A bishop is teacher in the diocese, helping people to grow in faith and be witnesses to Jesus. A bishop is shepherd in the diocese, caring for everyone, especially the poor. A bishop is bridge-builder in the diocese, uniting the community of Christians. In Latin, bridge-builder is *pontifex*. In English 'pontiff' is another word for 'bishop'. Each diocese has a cathedral, the bishop's official church. The name comes from the Greek word *cathedra*, meaning a chair or seat.

Find out the name of the diocese your school belongs to, its bishop or archbishop and where the cathedral is.

Extra!

- Find a map to show the Catholic dioceses of England and Wales. How many are there?
- ***Dioceses of England and Wales:*** *Copymaster* ☐3

Extra!

You are going to create a display for all Year 7 about local Catholic parishes. Display a large map of the local area.

1 ◆ Mark all the parishes that students in your class come from or live near.
2 ◆ Display photos of each member of the class and show which parish they attend or live near.
3 ◆ Display newsletters from these parishes, highlighting activities and events for young people.

Classwork

A new parish is being formed in your area. You are one of the following people: the priest, architect, a youth leader, the over 60s link worker, the president of the St Vincent de Paul Society, a CAFOD organiser.

A. *Prepare a two minute talk about your particular role. You will want the parishioners to know who you are, what you represent/do, how this contributes to the life of the parish and how they can be involved.*

B. *What will you want people to know about the new parish? Outline two or three ideas for a local publicity campaign. Use words and sketches.*

C. *It is the first Sunday Mass for the parish. You want everyone to feel welcome. Write a memo to explain who you would involve, where and when.*

The world-wide Church

Dioceses all over the world make up the *universal* or 'catholic' Church.

People of every nation belong to the Church. The bishop of Rome is called the Pope; the name means Father. In Italian 'father' is *papa*, in English – pope. The Pope is the head of the world-wide Catholic Church because he is the successor of St Peter. Jesus gave Peter responsibility for leading his Church. He called him the Rock on which his Church would stand. Peter and the other apostles spread the good news to all the nations of the world. Together the Pope, bishops and Christians everywhere continue the work of telling the good news to all the nations of the world.

universal: world-wide
catholic: 'universal', from the Greek word '*katholikos*'

Look at the photographs.
1. What do they tell you about the universal Catholic Church?
2. What is the name of the present Pope?
3. How long has he been Pope?
4. Use an encyclopedia or the Internet to find six facts about the Pope and the Vatican.
5. With a partner, prepare a question and answer quiz using the information you have discovered.

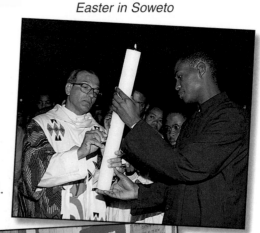

Easter in Soweto

a funeral in Panama

Mass in Brazil

Palm Sunday in the Philippines

Extra!

◆ Web activity: locate the website of a Catholic diocese or Catholic school in England or Wales. Use your ICT skills to create a promotion leaflet: why should someone visit this website? What will they enjoy or find useful?

Sharing the language of faith

Sunday unites the Church, 'the people God gathers'. It is the Lord's day and the Eucharist is the sacrament of thanksgiving and communion. In the actions and words of the Eucharist the Church *professes* its faith and *proclaims* the gospel.

to profess: to make a public statement, say what you believe openly
to proclaim: to make known, to announce

The Church

- **gathers** in the name of the Father, the Son and the Holy Spirit

- **proclaims** the Good News of God's love and faithfulness

- **professes** its faith in the words of the creed

- **gives thanks** for the life, death and resurrection of Jesus

- **shares** Jesus' offering of himself to the father and **receives** the gift of Jesus in holy communion

- is **sent** to live the good news God's people have celebrated, professed and proclaimed.

The Eucharist is commonly called Mass, from the Latin word *missa*, 'to be sent'. At the end of Mass the priest or deacon says: 'Go in peace and serve the Lord.'

Think and talk

What does the Sunday Eucharist tell you about what is important for the Church community?

Praying the Creed on Sunday is sharing words of faith that have been passed on from generation to generation.

Young people on retreat were asked to say in their own words what they believed. This is what some of them said:

> I believe that God loves each person individually.
> I believe that God sees everything we do.
> I believe that God forgives us.
> I believe that God is the true leader of mankind.
> I believe that the Mass is our offering to God.
>
> Andy

> I believe in my parents,
> my faith and God,
> the people who teach me,
> my friends, especially my best friend,
> love and honour;
> that there is more good than evil.
> God forgives people providing they are sorry.
>
> Anna

> I believe ... in people, in growing and learning, in love, in Christ, in nature.
>
> Donna

> I believe in the Almighty God our Creator, heaven and hell, my religion.
>
> Ged

Write your own 'I believe ...'

Homework

Words of faith: Copymasters [4] [5]

1A About belonging

Extra!

In 1982 Pope John Paul II came to Britain. In Cardiff he met some of the young people of England and Wales. Together they made a profession of faith.

Do you believe in God the Father?
We do believe. We accept God as Father and origin of life; creator and designer of all things. He is the source of all beauty and power who supports his people in justice and truth.

Do you believe in God the Son?
We do believe. We accept Jesus as the Christ, the Son of God, our brother and redeemer. He is our crucified and risen Lord, the Way of faith, the Truth of hope and the Life of love.

Do you believe in God the Holy Spirit?
We do believe. We accept the Spirit of God as the Giver of life, the bond of unity and peace. He is the Spirit of wisdom, the fire of perfect love who renews our minds and hearts.

Do you resolve to be God's people today and tomorrow?
We do resolve. We promise to listen to him in the community of the Church, to follow his ways and live in his love.

Do you resolve to live as God's people today and tomorrow?
We do resolve. We promise to respect all life as God's gift to us, to protect the right to life, and to promote especially the dignity, worth and wonder of each human person.

Do you resolve to share together your life as God's people today and tomorrow?
We do resolve. We promise to recognise all people as our brothers and sisters, to resist prejudice based on race, colour, or creed; to seek ways of living in harmony, unity and tolerance.

Do you resolve to work as God's people today and tomorrow?
We do resolve. We promise to co-operate in our work with God's creative design, to defend the right to useful and satisfying work, and to share the results of our labour, our possessions and our resources.

Do you resolve to seek peace as God's people today and tomorrow?
We do resolve. We promise to be peacemakers in the world in which we live; to turn aside from war and violence; to build God's kingdom where the poor and disadvantaged find hope and true justice.

Think and talk

1 ◆ What does the word 'believe' mean to you?

2 ◆ Belief will lead to action. What links can you find between the 'we believe' and 'we resolve' statements?

3 ◆ Choose one link that you think would most encourage young people and one that would be most challenging for them. With a partner, explain the reasons for your choice.

Making connections

Thought stop

Complete this sentence: Community is …

Testing times ❓

1. *Suggest two ways in which people can contribute to a parish community and explain what difference this contribution makes to parish life.*

2. *In your own words explain the two different meanings of the word 'church'.*

3. *What is the Local Church? What is the Universal Church?*

4. *What is the Creed and why is it said on Sundays?*

5. *What are a bishop's responsibilities? What are the Pope's responsibilities?*

Key words

For your Fact File:

community	**church**
parish	**universal**
diocese	**bishop**
Pope	**creed**

Pressure point
In or out? How do you know?

Words of faith

Try to find the rest of this hymn, and then choose another hymn about the Church used in your school liturgies and say why you like it. **Or** compose your own hymn based on what you have learned in this section of work.

Chorus We are companions on the journey, breaking bread and sharing life; and in the love we bear is the hope we share, for we believe in the love of our God.

No longer strangers to each other; no longer strangers in God's house; we are fed and we are nourished by the strength of those who care.

We have been gifted with each other, and we are called by the Word of the Lord: to act with justice, to love tenderly, and to walk humbly with our God.

Based on Micah 6:8; Matthew 7:7, Carey Landry

A matter of identity

In this section of our work we will be learning:

◆ what gives a community its special identity
◆ that the Church receives its identity from Jesus
◆ how to find your way around the Bible.

Our school community

Working in groups, look at your school's mission statement.

1. List three things it says about your school.
2. What links can you find between your work about community and the words of the mission statement?
3. Design an introduction to a two-page booklet for Year 6 students. You want them to know what is important and special about the school community they are joining and help them to settle in.

Or: Write a diary entry for one day at school from your arrival to departure. Make special note of anything that shows how the information in your booklet works out in practice.

Or: Design a 'pledge card'. On one side write the school's mission statement. On the other, write five pledges of ways in which students will behave, based on the mission statement.

Think and talk

What evidence can you find from your school mission statement and your school environment to show that Jesus has a special place in your school community?

Present your findings under a banner headline: JESUS MATTERS IN... and add the name of your school.

Check out what you know *Copymaster* [6] ✔
So you think you know Jesus

Without Jesus, no Church

The Church would not exist without Jesus. For 2,000 years people have put their faith in him. The Church believes Jesus is truly human and truly God. He is sent by God his Father to bring good news. Let's look at the evidence.

When people met Jesus in around AD 30, they saw a man. When he walked into a room, people did not think he was God. It took those who knew him best a long time to work out that he was the Son of God.

The Church's earliest historical documents are the letters of St Paul. In about AD 56, less than thirty years after the death and resurrection of Jesus, Paul writes to the Church at Philippi saying that, at the name of Jesus, everyone 'will fall on their knees and all will openly proclaim that Jesus Christ is *Lord* to the glory of God the Father.' (Philippians 2:10–11)

About thirty years later the gospel of John *proclaims*: 'We saw his glory, the glory which he received as the Father's only Son.' (John 1:14)

proclaim: make known
Lord : at the time of Jesus, a title for someone who had total authority

The Gospels: Four portraits of Jesus

You could say the gospels are the Church's 'mission statement'. They proclaim what the Church believes about the message and mission of Jesus. The gospels were not written as biographies. They were written to tell the good news of Jesus Christ, the Son of God, by writers who wanted their readers to share their faith in Jesus. The gospels are part of the New Testament.

The four Evangelists from the Lindisfarne Gospels:

Matthew

Mark

Luke

John

Words we use

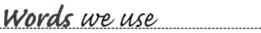

evangelist – gospel writer, from the Greek *evangelion*, meaning 'good news'
gospel – from the Anglo-Saxon *godespel*, meaning 'good news'

1

The New Testament is Part Two of the Christian Bible. Part One is the Old Testament, which tells the story of God's love and special relationship with the Jewish people. It was written before the birth of Jesus. Christians read it as the story of God's preparation for the coming of Jesus. The Church believes that those who wrote all the books of the Bible, both Old and New Testament, were *inspired* by the Spirit of God. This means that what they wrote would faithfully *reveal* the truth about who God is.

inspired: specially guided by the Holy Spirit
reveal: make known, show, make visible

Bible skills

Finding your way around the Bible needs special skills.
Copymasters 7 8

What was Jesus like?

Jesus was human. He grew from a baby to an adult. He learned to walk and talk. He made friends. He got tired and hungry. He cried when his friend died. He was frightened about the future. Just like us, he learned and grew in understanding. (Luke 2:52)

Look at three passages: Luke 8:22–25; John 11:35; Mark 14:33–35.
1 What do they tell you about the kind of man Jesus was?
2 What do you think the people with him thought and felt about him?
3 What questions might they have wanted to ask Jesus

Miracles

The gospels tell of the miracles of Jesus. The miracles are signs that reveal who Jesus is. When people saw miracles they wondered about Jesus. 'Who is he?' they asked. When they listened to him they were amazed. He taught and acted with confidence and authority.

Look at these three passages: Mark 3:1–7; Luke 8:22–25; Luke 13:10–17.
1. What do you think the people with Jesus thought?
2. What do you think they said about him?
3. What questions might they have wanted to ask Jesus?

☰ Homework 🏛 ☰

On the Map Copymaster 9

Thought stop

At the end of his gospel John wrote: 'Now there are many other things that Jesus did. If they were all written down one by one, I suppose that the whole world could not hold the books that would be written.' (John 21:25)

Portrait of Jesus

The gospels do not tell us what Jesus looked like, but artists through the centuries have tried to portray him.

Look at the pictures.

1. What do you think each artist is trying to say about Jesus?
2. Collect some images of Jesus. You might do this from books in the library or RE department, from pictures or statues of Jesus in the school or in church, from videos about Jesus or from the Internet.
3. Which do you think best portrays Jesus as he is described in the gospel passages you have read?

Classwork ✍

A profile of Jesus

A. Select two or three pieces of information from the work you have done. Explain what they tell us about Jesus and why you have chosen them.

B. Use the work you have done to design a poster or profile page about Jesus to post on a website or send to a pen-friend who has never heard about Jesus. Your aim is to encourage your readers to want to find out more about Jesus.

C. From the work you have done, identify some words, phrases or actions of Jesus that might make people ask the question: Who is he? What does the telling of these events show about the evangelists' faith that Jesus is truly human and truly God?

1B A matter of identity

Making connections

Thought stop

What have you understood about your school's mission statement?

What have you learned about Jesus' mission?

Testing times ?

1. What is the difference between the Old and New Testament in the Christian Bible?

2. What are the gospels? Name the four evangelists.

3. Name one other book from the New Testament and one from the Old Testament.

4. Find different ways of expressing the following:

   (a) John 1:14

   (b) Luke 12:13–20

   (c) 1 Corinthians 13:4

   (d) 1 Samuel 3:1–16

5. What have you learned about Jesus from your work with the gospels in this section?

Pressure point

A stranger visits your school. How would he or she know that Jesus is special to your school community?

Words of faith

At the name of Jesus
every knee shall bow,
every tongue confess him
King of glory now;
'tis the Father's pleasure
we should call him Lord,
who from the beginning,
was the mighty Word.

Caroline Noel (1817–77)

Key *words*

For your Fact File:

gospel
mission
inspired
New Testament
Old Testament
proclaim
miracle
evangelist

Find a twentieth-century hymn or song of praise of Jesus used in your school liturgies that you like. Why have you chosen it?

Compose a hymn about Jesus for the twenty-first century.

Thought stop

The face of Christ

The story goes that Leonardo da Vinci was looking for a model for the figure of Jesus in his painting of the Last Supper. He was not satisfied with anyone he saw. Then one day he saw a young man whose face was open and honest. Quickly he made a sketch. 'This is the face of Christ for my painting,' he thought.

Leonardo's great painting took years to complete. At last, the only figure left to do was Judas, the disciple who betrayed Jesus. Leonardo searched the faces of people in the streets. He looked in bars and inns all over the town. One night he saw a man in a bar. 'This is it,' he thought, 'the face of a betrayer.' He began to sketch. Little by little his artist's eye began to recognise something familiar in the shape of the man's face and head. Suddenly he stopped. This was the man he had drawn years before. It was the face he had given Christ in his picture.

1B A matter of identity

1C Living relationships

Choose one scenario to improvise.

Scenario 1

A newcomer has a very different accent from the local one which everyone else in the class uses. Improvise two situations:

1. welcome, acceptance and how the newcomer might make a difference
2. unfriendly response, the newcomer not accepted.

In each case show how the situation affects the newcomer, individuals in the class and the whole class.

Scenario 2

Someone returns after being excluded for a week for bullying.

Improvise one or more moments of the firstday back. How is he or she accepted back? How does this affect the person, the people who were bullied, and the whole class?

Think and talk

In each of the scenarios, how did the situations affect relationships? Identify some positive and negative changes.

Thought stop

Relationships matter

Relationships are important for individuals and communities. Draw a spider diagram with yourself in the middle. Around you write the names of people who are important in your life.

Work with a partner.

1. Share your spider diagrams. Why did you choose these people?

2. In what ways are they important to you?

3. How would you be different if you had never known them?

4. Name some positive ways you have made a difference to these people's lives.

5. What do you think these people would say about what you mean to them?

Check out what you know ✔

At film and TV award ceremonies winners try to thank everyone, from their families to the budgie! Who would you want to thank?

What might a Christian say about thanking Jesus?

> **In this section of our work we will be learning:**
> - about the importance of relationships in community
> - that Jesus calls people to a communion that is sharing the life of God.

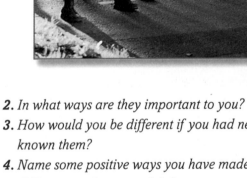

Come follow me

For Christians, relationship with Jesus is *vital*. Two thousand years ago in Palestine Jesus called people to live in relationship with him, with God his Father and with one another. The New Testament also shows how his call and challenge continues after his death and resurrection.

vital: full of life, essential for life

Meet Levi

I was a tax collector. Nobody wanted to know me. OK, I may have pushed people around a bit but a man's gotta make a living. I hate crowds. I feel under pressure. I know people don't like me.

I was sitting there with people crowding round me, all complaining. Jesus passed by. Through the crowd he caught my eye. He just said, 'Follow me!'

And do you know what? I did. I just stood up and walked after him.

Meet Philip and Nathanael

I'm Philip. When I met Jesus and he said 'Follow me,' I didn't think twice. I just went with him. My friend Nathanael was different. When I told him about Jesus he asked 'Where is he from?' When I said Nazareth, he nearly died. 'Nazareth!' he said, 'Can anything good come from Nazareth?' But when he met Jesus, things were different. Jesus said to him, 'You're an honest man!' Nathanael was amazed. He said afterwards that it felt like Jesus was looking right into his heart. Now we both follow Jesus.

Not everybody who met Jesus responded so positively. Here's Levi again.

I was so happy to know Jesus that I threw a party. I wanted people to know him. The guest list included several tax collectors and others who wouldn't get many invitations to dinner. The local religious leaders watched the guests arrive and they were not impressed. They muttered about it and criticised Jesus. 'What's he doing eating with those kinds of people? Doesn't he know what they are like?'

Do you know, Jesus didn't have a problem. He said these were just the kind of people he wanted to meet. His good news was especially for them. By the way, I changed my name as well as my way of life. Now I'm called Matthew.

He's from where?

Meet Saul

I'm Saul. I was against the new Christians. I did my best to get them thrown into prison. Then one day, on the way to Damascus, everything changed in a flash. I heard Jesus speak to me as clear as could be. He said, 'Saul, Saul! Why do you persecute me?' 'Who are you, Lord?' I asked. 'I am Jesus of Nazareth, whom you persecute,' he said to me. The men with me saw the light, but did not hear the voice. I asked, 'What shall I do?' and the Lord said to me, 'Get up and go into Damascus, and there you will be told what God wants you to do.' So I did as I was told. A disciple called Ananias baptised me and taught me about Jesus. I knew God wanted me to be a disciple and spread the gospel of Jesus. Now I use my Greek name, Paul, instead of my Jewish name, Saul.

Meet Lydia

*I'm Lydia. I live in Philippi. One **Sabbath** day I went to pray with the other Jews. We used to meet on the river bank. Paul and his companions came along and started talking to us about Jesus. His words touched my heart and I knew God was calling me to believe in Jesus and be baptised. Paul baptised me and also my family, servants and workers. I make and sell purple cloth. Dying the cloth is a skilled job and I am well known for the quality of my work. I invited Paul and his friends to stay at my house. They stayed with us until some people stirred up trouble and they were arrested. But that's another story.*

Sabbath: the Jewish holy day, our Saturday

Disciples

Luke's gospel tells how men and women who answered Jesus' call became disciples. (Luke 8:1–3). Disciples share the life of a teacher or leader because they want to live like that person. Jesus' disciples listened to him. They watched how he treated people. They shared their fears with him. They ate with him. They saw him tired. They saw him happy. At the end of all this Jesus said, 'I've shared everything with you, about my Father, about what is right, about the good news that brings life and happiness to every kind of person. You know me and I know you. You are my friends. Everyone will know you are my friends if you love one another.'

John's gospel sums up the call of Jesus like this:

I give you a new commandment:
Love one another;
Just as I have loved you,
You also must love one another.
By this love you have for one another,
Everyone will know that you are my disciples.

(John 13:34–35)

A sign for the world

Jesus did not just call people to be disciples 2000 years ago. He continues to call people to be disciples. The Church is the community of disciples who answer Jesus' call to live in *communion* with him, with God his Father and with each other.

God's life is a communion of three persons – The Father, the Son and the Holy Spirit. The three persons, the Trinity, share their life and love so perfectly that the Three are One. This is One of the deepest *mysteries* of Christian faith.

This communion is a sign for the world. It proclaims what God is and what it means to be human. Relationships are very important for people. The Church believes that this is because people are created in the image of God. They are created for communion.

Communion: loving relationship through Jesus with one another and the Father and the Holy Spirit

mystery: something that takes us beyond human understanding

One way of thinking about this loving communion is to study some of Jesus' words in John's gospel:

> I pray not only for these, but also for those who believe in me because of their message. I pray that they may all be one. Father! May they be one in us, just as you are in me and I am in you. May they be one so that the world will believe that you sent me. *(John 17:20–21)*

> I am the vine and you are the branches. Whoever remains in me and I in him will bear much fruit; for you can do nothing without me.' *(John 15:5)*

Classwork

A. Prepare some questions you would like to ask one of the disciples whose story you heard. Ask for volunteers to sit in the 'hot seat' and answer the questions as the disciples.

B. Research a modern disciple, someone who is trying to live as a follower of Jesus today. Hint: it could be the person next door! Include in your report: why he or she is a disciple; how they try to follow Jesus; what makes them happy about being a disciple and what they find difficult.

Prepare a 'testimony' (witness statement) to give to the class about how Jesus called you and changed your life.

C. Jesus uses the image of the vine and the branches to describe his relationship with his followers. Read it in John 15:5. What does this image say to you about the privilege and the responsibility of being a disciple? Think of another image to describe Jesus' relationship with his disciples. Present your image in a way of your choice.

Homework

One year on

You are a reporter on the Galilee Chronicle. You are following up people one year on from a meeting with Jesus that changed their lives. Choose one person and write a story for a young people's magazine. Points to include: what is the person doing now; how have they changed; how have their relationships with others changed.

Or Imagine Jesus has come to your neighbourhood. Who would he call to be disciples today? How do you think people would respond?

1C Living relationships

Portraits of disciples

Jesus said: 'Everyone will know that you are my disciples if you love one another.' Christian disciples show their love for God and for one another in many different ways.

Disciples: past ...

Julian of Norwich

Julian lived in Norwich over six hundred years ago. She was an anchoress who lived in a special cell attached to the parish church of St Julian. She was the first woman to write a book in English. Her hermit's cell had one window that opened onto the inside of the church and the altar, and another that opened onto the street for those who came to her wanting advice or a listening ear. This icon shows her at the outside window with her cat, ready to listen.

... and present

Martyrs of the Jesuit University (El Salvador)

These six priests and two women were murdered in El Salvador's civil war. They were teachers, priests, peace-makers, innocent women. Their crime was to try to live the gospel and to stand up for the democratic rights of their fellow citizens. They gave their lives so that the ideals they cherished would not die.

Think and talk

1. In what ways do these disciples show what is holy in human life?
2. How do they show, by their actions, what they believe?
3. Interview a Christian disciple and report back to your class. Why is faith important to them? What difference does it make to their lives? What opportunities do they have to show love for Jesus and others?

A community called L'Arche (The Ark)

People in L'Arche community

Choose a group to visit the *L'Arche* website. Select information to download for the class.

Fact file:

Beginnings

where	France
when	1964
who	Jean Vanier and Father Thomas Phillippe.
how	Jean invited two men with learning difficulties to live with him in the first *L'Arche* community.
why	To live like Jesus, in the spirit of the gospel, to make a place for everyone.

Today

where	All over the world.
who	People with and without special physical or learning needs. Volunteer helpers come for a year or more.
how	Sharing their differences, making a home together, sharing work, leisure and prayer.
why	To build a community in which everyone contributes something; to grow in communion with each other and with Jesus; to build a community that offers a real home.

Making connections

Thought stop

A headteacher used to say this to the first Year 7 assembly of each year:

'This school will never be the same again because of each one of you.'

What do you think she was saying about each person's relationship with the school community? What do you think she was saying about the community's relationship with each person?

Key *words*

For your Fact File:

- disciple
- call
- privilege
- responsibility
- L'Arche
- relationships

Testing times ?

1. Name two people who responded to Jesus' call. How were their lives changed?
2. What was Jesus' call about?
3. What image did Jesus use for his relationship with his disciples?
4. What does the word L'Arche mean? What is its vision?
5. What are some signs of being a disciple?

Pressure point

Felistus' story

Felistus Jere's school is a grim patch of wasteland. The dirt on the ground is her blackboard. Her teacher is an unpaid volunteer. As Felistus carefully scratches out numbers, the wind picks up the dirt and hurls it into her eyes. What might the Christian response be to Felistus?

Words of faith

Lord Jesus Christ,
Friend and Brother,
May we know you more clearly,
Love you more dearly,
And follow you more nearly.

What does this say about being a disciple of Jesus?

This is the prayer of Richard of Chichester (1197–1253). It was used as the inspiration for a song in the musical *Godspell*. Find the song and listen to it.

1C Living relationships

1D Celebrating initiation

Welcome

Mary was one of 180 new Year 7 pupils at St Michael's Catholic School. As she waited in the hall with the other pupils for assembly she felt a little lonely and quite scared. She felt that she knew no one. Everyone looked the same in the school uniform. The headteacher welcomed them all to the school. He introduced the head of Year 7 and all the form teachers. He told them that this was an important day for them all.

'Today marks a new stage in your life. It is a new start for each of you. I hope that you will make the most of the opportunities that you will have here and that you will be happy.'

1. Imagine you are Mary's form teacher. What would you do next to help Mary and her class settle in to the new school? What will make them feel at home?
2. Think back to your first weeks in this school. Make a list of Do's and Don'ts for welcoming new students. Compare your answers with at least one other person.

Just one stage

Mary's headteacher said she was beginning a new stage in her life. 'It's a new start,' he said. Draw a timeline to show some stages that led up to Mary's first day at school.

Mark some of the stages that may be still to come. This illustration has some ideas to help you.

Extra!

1 ♦ Which events could be the start of other 'journeys'?
2 ♦ Which events do you think mark stages in Mary's Christian journey?
3 ♦ What stages are still to come?

Initiation: learning to belong

Learning to belong to a community takes time. Signs, symbols and rituals can help people to learn about the community and share its life.

1. Use the work you have done so far to list the special signs, symbols and rituals that were used to help you become part of your school community.
2. What other experiences of welcome or initiation have you had?
3. What signs, symbols and rituals were used?

Words we use

sign – a notice or object that points the way and gives names, such as shop names, road signs;

– a uniform can also be a sign; for example fire officer, school uniform

ritual – action that is a regular part of a person's life, such as brushing teeth;

– action that has a regular place and meaning in an event, such as exchanging pennants at the start of an international game;

– action that has a regular place in worship, such as blessing with holy water

rite – way an event is celebrated by a community, such as an initiation ceremony

symbol – an object which carries a special meaning for a person or a community, such as a wedding ring, school badge; an action that has a special meaning, such as a handshake;

– an object which carries a religious meaning, for example a crucifix, incense

Gifts of God

The Catholic Church celebrates stages of Christian life with seven sacraments. The actions and words of each sacramental celebration are a meeting that takes the form of a dialogue between God and the Christian disciple. Each sacrament deepens the relationship of the disciple with God and with the Church.

Check Out What You Know *Gifts of God* Copymaster

Sacraments of initiation

Baptism, Confirmation and the Eucharist are the three sacraments of initiation into the Catholic Christian community. They are the beginning of the disciple's life in communion with Jesus Christ and the Church.

The Catholic Church celebrates initiation with different rites. The photographs show two Catholic families at the baptism of their babies. One family is celebrating in the Roman or Latin rite, and one in the Eastern rite.

Immersion is used in the Eastern rite.

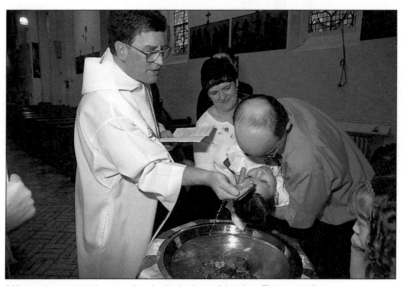

Water is poured over the baby's head in the Roman rite.

The Roman Catholic baby will be baptised, but it will be a number of years before his Christian initiation is completed. He will celebrate the other two sacraments of initiation separately.

For the other baby there will be a single celebration of the three sacraments of Christian initiation.

The Church in England and Wales follows the Roman rite.

Think and talk

1. What will the next stage of their Christian journey be for the two babies?
2. How will they be similar?
3. How will they be different?

Focus on Baptism in the Roman rite

Even in the Roman rite Baptism is celebrated in different ways:
during Mass, at the Easter Vigil or in a separate ceremony. We
will be studying the separate ceremony so that we can focus
on the signs and symbols used and their meaning.

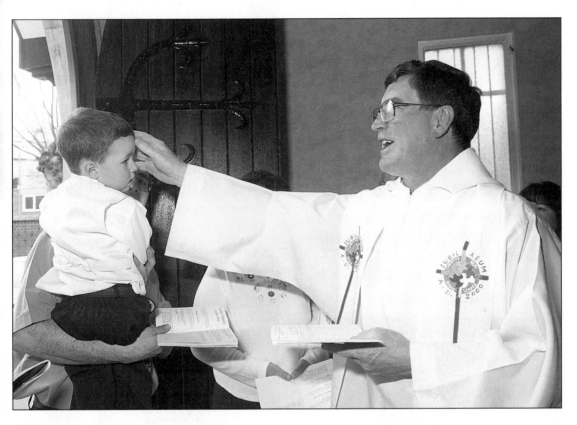

Welcome: at the door

The Church gathers. The baby is welcomed by name.
A name is a sign of belonging.

Priest: *What name have you given your child?*

Parents: *Patrick Daniel*

Priest: *What do you ask of God's Church?*

Parents: *Baptism*

Priest: *Patrick Daniel, the Christian community welcomes you
with great joy. In its name I claim you for Christ our
Saviour by the sign of his cross. I now trace the sign of
the cross on your forehead and invite your parents and
godparents to do the same.*

The Word of God: at the lectern

The Word of God is
proclaimed: a sign that the
new disciple is called to
hear and live the good news
of Jesus.

1D Celebrating initiation

Baptism: at the font

1. The priest or deacon anoints Patrick Daniel with the oil of baptism. It is a sign of strength. Christ will strengthen Patrick Daniel to reject evil and choose what is good.

2. The parents and godparents are invited to renew their baptismal promises. They renounce evil and express their faith in God the Father, Son and Holy Spirit. The water of Baptism is blessed.

3.

Patrick Daniel, I baptise you in the name of the Father, and of the Son and of the Holy Spirit.

4.

See in this white garment the outward sign of your Christian dignity.

5. The anointing with the oil of chrism is a sign that, in the eyes of God the Father, the new disciple shares Christ's mission as priest, prophet and king. He is called to live in communion with him for ever.

6.

Receive the light of Christ. Parents and godparents, this light is entrusted to you to be kept burning brightly. This child of yours has been enlightened by Christ. He is to walk always as a child of the light.

Communion of Life: at the altar

The family gathers around the altar. The priest or deacon reminds the family that Patrick Daniel's initiation will be completed by the sacraments of Confirmation and Eucharist. Together everyone prays the Our Father. It is a sign that Patrick Daniel is a member of the Church in communion with Jesus and all baptised Christians.

Looking forward

Patrick Daniel's journey of Christian initiation will be completed by the sacraments of Confirmation and the Eucharist. At Confirmation the laying on of hands symbolises the coming of the Holy Spirit. In the sacrament of the Eucharist Patrick Daniel will receive the Body and Blood of Christ. (You will be studying Confirmation and Eucharist in more detail later in *Icons*.)

Classwork ✎

Celebrating Baptism

A. *Make a baptism card. You must include at least one symbol, one action and some words to show the meaning of Baptism.*

B. *Design four modern windows for a baptistry. Include the signs, symbols and steps of the rite. Use these titles for each stage: Welcome (door); Word of God (book); Baptism with water (font); One family (altar).*

C. *Baptism means…*
Choose one stage of the celebration of Baptism and write a short presentation about its place and importance in the ceremony and in people's lives.

Homework 🏛

The sign of the Christian

Look at the pictures.

1. *What do these crosses say to you about Jesus and about being a disciple?*

2. *The cross forms a basic shape in many designs. Create your own design pattern using a cross shape. Include the word 'Jesus' in your pattern if you can.*

1D Celebrating initiation

Making connections

Thought stop

'It takes time to belong.' What do you think?

Testing times ❓

1. *What is a sacrament?*
2. *What are the three sacraments of initiation of the Catholic Church?*
3. *Name two symbols used in Baptism. Write a sentence for each to explain their meaning.*
4. *When is the Sign of the Cross used in the rite of Baptism?*
5. *In your own words describe some of the privileges and responsibilities that Christian baptism brings.*

Pressure point

Is it possible to tell a baptised person from a person who has not been baptised?

Words of faith

Do not be afraid, for I have redeemed you.
I have called you by your name; you are mine.

You are mine, O my child, I am your Father,
and I love you with a perfect love.

Gerald Markland, based on Isaiah 54:1–4

What does this hymn say about God's call and a disciple's response?

Present your answer in your own words, another hymn or song, a prayer, a piece of art or a photograph.

Key *words*
. . . .

For your Fact File:

initiation
journey
ritual
sacrament
symbol
sign
rite
Baptism

Celebrating Christ's Mass

Time after time

Times and seasons affect us all. Morning, afternoon, evening and night: every day has its pattern. Spring, summer, autumn, winter: the seasons of the year follow their cycle.

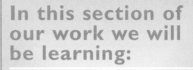

In this section of our work we will be learning:

◆ about the importance of times and seasons in our lives
◆ about the times and seasons of the Christian calendar
◆ that at Chrismas the Church celebrates the Word made flesh and Mary's role in the Christmas event.

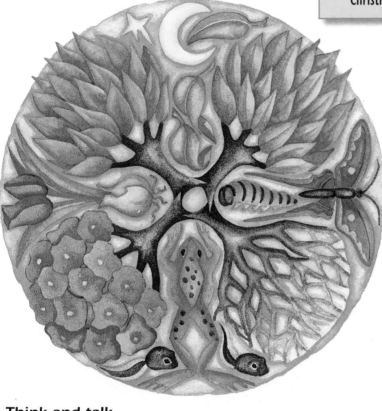

Think and talk

1. Look at the illustration. Identify as many different times, seasons and cycles as you can.
2. Describe the season you like best and say what makes it special for you.
3. Seasons are not the only way we divide time. Name some other ways.

Extra!

Design two calendars: one for general use and one for school use. Make differences and similarities clear. Discuss your ideas with a partner.

Words we use

calendar – a set period of time such as a year, a school year, Christian year, farming year – a way of measuring time such as a wall calendar for months, a diary for weeks

seasons – different parts of a calendar period such as spring, harvest, Christmas

cycle – a regular pattern marking times such as day and night, seasons of the year, Christian feasts, generations

Calendars

People follow different calendars. For many people the beginning of the New Year is January. The beginning of the school year is September. For each person a birthday is the beginning of a new year. The Christian Church has its own calendar of feasts and seasons. It takes its shape from the life, death and resurrection of Jesus.

Check out what you know ☑

Match the major feasts and seasons with the thing they celebrate.

Pentecost	the coming of Jesus
Lent	Jesus: new life, new beginning
Christmas	the gift of the Holy Spirit
Easter	a Saviour is born
Advent	time to change and follow Jesus

It's Christmas!

Look at a variety of Christmas cards.
What messages about Christmas do they give?
What different ways of celebrating Christmas do they show?
What kind of Christmas celebrations do they encourage?
Share your thoughts with at least one other person.

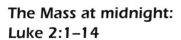

1

Christ's Mass: good news of God's gift of Jesus

The word 'Christmas' comes from the words 'The Mass of Christ's birth'. It was shortened to 'Christ's Mass' and then to 'Christmas'. It is the Church's celebration of the birth of Jesus, a joyful celebration of his coming. It is a thanksgiving celebration because the Son of God is sent to the world.

It is the only feast in the Church's year that has three special Masses. Together they tell the story of Jesus and his mission. Tell each gospel story in your own words trying to include all the key words given here.

The Mass at midnight:
Luke 2:1–14

census
Joseph and Mary
town of David
son
angel messenger
shepherds
Christ the Lord

The Mass at dawn:
Luke 2:15–20

angels
shepherds
Bethlehem
Mary and Joseph
the baby lying in the manger
praising God

The Mass during the day:
John 1:1–14

Word	beginning
life	light
darkness	overcome
John	world
God the Father	children of God
Word made flesh	Son
glory	

Use your Bible skills to find the gospel passages and check your answers.

Luke's message

What does Luke want people to picture? What does he want them to know about Jesus?

Can you find the Christmas carol that begins 'It came upon a midnight clear'? Luke's gospel does not say anything about midnight. Why do you think Midnight Mass is traditional? Some parishes now have 'Midnight' Mass at 8pm. Why do you think this is happening? What is your opinion? Give your reasons.

The **Word** was made **flesh**.

John's message

What does John want people to know about Jesus?

What does John want people to know about themselves?

Which phrase expresses John's faith that God the Son was born a human baby?

Work in groups

1 ◆ Find a Christmas carol to match one gospel account of the birth of Jesus.
2 ◆ What line of the carol sums up the gospel story best? You might like to share your findings in song.

Extra!

The Church's Christmas celebrations are about welcoming Jesus. In the three gospels you have read, how many different welcomes can you find?

We use words

We use words to express ourselves.

Words may be spoken. Written words are silent. Actions can be words: a nod for 'yes', a shake of the head for 'no'. Words give shape, in sound, to our thoughts. They 'flesh out' what we think and mean. The Church believes that Jesus is the living Word of God. Everything that God the Father wants to say is expressed in Jesus. John's gospel says 'The Word was made flesh'. The Church's word for this is *incarnation* – in the flesh.

Homework 🏛

Getting the message

Choose two or three Christmas cards that you think express the real message of Christmas. Stick them into your book or reproduce them using ICT. Write about one of them. Why do you think it gives the real message of Christmas?

Most highly favoured lady

Mary is the mother of Jesus. The Church believes that Mary is blessed because of the role she agreed to play in God's plan. The Church honours her as mother of Jesus and therefore Mother of God.

Classwork

A. *Hail Mary*

Read the Hail Mary and the carol.

Copy down words or phrases that you most like.

Why do you like them?

What do these prayers tell you about what the Church believes about Mary?

Hail Mary, full of grace,
The Lord is with you.
Blessed are you among women
and blessed is the fruit of your womb, Jesus.
Holy Mary, Mother of God,
pray for us sinners,
now and at the hour of our death.
Amen.

Gabriel's Message

The angel Gabriel, from heaven came,
His wings as drifted snow, his eyes as flame.
'All hail,' said he, 'thou lowly maiden, Mary!
Most highly favoured lady! Gloria!'

'For know, a blessed mother thou shalt be,
All generations laud and honour thee.
Thy son shall be Emmanuel by seers foretold.
Most highly favoured lady! Gloria!'

Then gentle Mary meekly bowed her head.
'To me be, as it pleaseth God,' she said.
'My soul shall laud and magnify his holy name!'
Most highly favoured lady! Gloria!

Of her, Emmanuel, the Christ was born
In Bethlehem all on a Christmas morn;
And Christian folk throughout the world will ever say:
'Most highly favoured lady! Gloria!'

Sabine Baring–Gould

B. *God's message*

Read the Hail Mary and Gabriel's Message again.

Write, in your own words, Gabriel's message and Mary's response.

C. *Annunciation*

Read Luke 1: 26–38 – The Annunciation of the Lord

1. What is Luke's message about Jesus?

2. What is Luke's message about Mary?

3. What is Luke's message about God?

1E Celebrating Christ's Mass

Making connections

Thought stop

"Put Christ back into Christmas!"

Testing times ?

1. When does the Church's year begin?
2. Name three seasons of the Church's year.
3. Name three major feasts and explain how they celebrate Jesus.
4. What is one title that shows the Church honours Mary?
5. Write two sentences to explain what Christians celebrate at Christmas.

Pressure point

'Many people these days do not believe in Christ at all. It's time to change the name of the festival to Gift-Time.' What do you think?

No room at the inn: crisis at Christmas

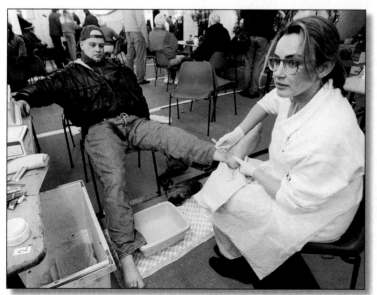

A shelter run by Crisis offers care for the homeless over Christmas. Who else makes room at Christmas?

Think wider

How is Christmas celebrated in other parts of the world?

For your Fact File:

Christmas

cycle

season

Mary

liturgical year

Word made flesh

Emmanuel

carol

Jesus the Saviour

Check out what you know ✓

'Today a Saviour has been born for you. He is Christ the Lord.'

In this section of our work we will be learning:

◆ about some needs and wants in our lives and the difference between them
◆ that the gospel proclaims Jesus is the One who saves from sin and death.

If you had to explain to a Year 2 pupil what Jesus came to do, what would you say? Keep it simple.

Think and talk

1. 'Jesus is the number one Christmas present.' True or false? Why, or why not?
2. Make a list of Christmas presents 11 or 12-year-olds might have received or given.
3. Divide them into what they might need and what they might want.
4. Think about presents you have received or given. Did you ever get a present that someone thought you needed? How do you decide what present to give? Did you ever give a present because someone really needed it? Did you ever give a present because you thought someone really wanted it? Listen to what others say.
5. What have you learned about the difference between what people 'need' and 'want'? Summarise your findings in a short paragraph.

Think wider

Look at the photographs. What different needs and wants might these people have?

What happens when needs and wants cannot be met?
Where do people go?
Share your ideas with the class.

Thought stop

Help God!

A 1997 survey found that 87 per cent of people said that they would pray in times of stress or trouble. People seem to need a God who will listen and help. A 1999 survey found that 23 per cent of 18–24-year-olds see themselves as Christians.

Unit 2 Christ the Light

God's answer

The Church believes that God's answer is Jesus. Matthew's gospel (1:18–21) tells us that God named Mary's baby 'Jesus'. In Hebrew the name means 'God saves'. The Hebrew form of his name is 'Yeshua'. In English there are two versions of 'Yeshua': Joshua and Jesus.

The gospels show Jesus as someone who is clear about his *mission*. He is sent by God his Father to bring good news of God's love to the poor. In his words and actions he reveals God's power to save, to heal and to forgive. He never gives up on his mission. He is obedient to his death on the cross and by his faithfulness he overcomes sin and death. His death brings *salvation*. Use your Bible skills to look at the evidence.

salvation: God's actions that save people; God's love that saves, rescues and gives life

mission: one task or job; a person's main work in life; what Jesus came to do

File 2

Mark 2:1–12
Forgiveness and healing

THE NEWS ABOUT JESUS SPREAD VERY QUICKLY

Why did people come to Jesus?
What did they hope to get?
What did Jesus give?

File 1

Luke 4:16–21
A public beginning

JESUS MAKES A PUBLIC ANNOUNCEMENT ABOUT HIS MISSION IN HIS HOME TOWN

What does Jesus say about his mission?

LEARNING RESOURCES CENTRE
John Paul II School

File 4

Luke 23:39–43
God's saving love

TWO CRIMINALS WERE CRUCIFIED WITH JESUS, ONE ON EITHER SIDE OF HIM

What made one change?
What did he ask of Jesus?
What did Jesus promise?

File 3

Luke 22:14–16, 19–20
The cost of the mission

AT THE END, JESUS' LOVE FOR HIS FATHER AND FOR OTHERS COST HIM EVERYTHING

How did Jesus give everything?
What happened the next day?

Thought stop

'Dying he destroyed our death;
rising he restored our life.'

Classwork

A. Select one file. On one side of A4 paper, create a six-frame story to describe Jesus' mission. Include: what Jesus said, the people he met; what he did: and what people thought.

B. Copy the quotation from the prophet Isaiah in Luke's gospel referred to in File 1. What evidence can you offer that this passage did come true? Use work you have done about Jesus in this section or in 1A. Give at least five pieces of evidence.

C. Look back to your work on Think wider on page 41. How do you think faith in Jesus as Saviour could help in these situations? Choose one of them. Describe the need, and explain how you think faith in Jesus might bring about a change and help people.

The Gospel challenge

Jesus' death devastated his disciples. Risen from the dead, Jesus himself showed them that his death was part of his saving mission. This is the good news that the Church tries to live and proclaim in action so that all people will hear it. This is the challenge for all Christians.

Lent is the season when the Church says to Christians: 'Come on! Look at how you are living. Look at how you need Jesus to help you to meet this challenge.'

Ash Wednesday marks the beginning of six weeks of Lent. Christians are signed with the sign of the cross using ashes. The ashes are a symbol of time passing and death. The cross is a symbol of how Jesus gave his life for all people. As they receive the ashes, each person is challenged to 'Turn away from sin and be faithful to the gospel'. Lenten tradition challenges the Church to do this in three ways:

Fasting

This is not just about not eating food or giving up sweets. It is about making time and space for God and for self-denial – saying 'no' to self and 'yes' to the gospel.

Almsgiving

This means giving help in the form of money and thinking especially of those in need. It is a challenge to act justly. CAFOD holds a Fast Day and an envelope collection on the second Friday of Lent.

Prayer

The aim of all Lenten self-denial is to draw closer to God. Time for prayer is time for God.

Work as a class

1 ◆ Use the work you have already done about Jesus and the gospel to suggest some Lenten challenges that will help Christians to 'Turn away from sin and be faithful to the gospel'.
2 ◆ Use some of these ideas to make a 'Lent Reminder' for your class or year group. Display it before and during Lent. You could have one thought for each week, or one for each day.

Homework

Jesus said: 'If you want to be my disciple you must deny yourself, take up your cross and follow me.' Why would someone say 'Yes' or 'No' to the challenge? Expain in two paragraphs titled 'Yes' and 'No'.

Thought stop

As old as the hills

Throughout history, people have used fasting to focus their minds, to get closer to God, to grow in self-control or draw attention to injustice. People of all religions understand the power of fasting. During Lent, Christians fast or give up things they like to eat. Jewish people fast in the days running up to the festival of Yom Kippur. The followers of Islam fast from sunrise to dusk for a whole month during the annual feast of Ramadan. In a world where one-fifth of the people consume most of the world's resources while others go hungry, fasting is a powerful statement.

Proclaim the Good News

The good news is not just for Lent. For many people good news begins with justice. CAFOD is the Catholic Agency For Overseas Development and Rosa is one of the people in the developing world for whom CAFOD works.

Rosa wants a job

'I'm looking for work but can't find it,' Rosa told CAFOD. 'I will do anything, but it's very hard to make ends meet.'

On the third day her family had gone without food, 18-year-old Rosa felt forced to go back on the streets. Without any money coming in to feed her mother and six brothers and sisters, there seemed to be no alternative.

Her father had left the family years earlier. Until recently, her mother had a job working in the kitchen of the university, but she lost it in the last round of government spending cuts. With 70 per cent unemployment, it has proved impossible for either Rosa or her mother to find work.

Rosa and her family live in Lomalinda, a shanty area on the outskirts of Managua, the capital of Nicaragua. Their house, reached by a dirt road, has no running water and they must fetch water each day from the nearest standpipe. The floors inside are bare concrete.

'We're desperate,' says Rosa's mother, Maria. 'We have no rice to eat. I can't afford shoes or new clothes for my children. We can see no solution. We rely on what help we can get from the base Christian community.'

Supported by CAFOD, Father Arnaldo Zenteno organises community kitchens, or *ollas*, which provide food for under-fives and breast-feeding mothers. There is also skills training for girls at risk of involvement in prostitution.

Here Rosa is now learning to type, to sew and to work in the kitchen. She hopes these skills will help her find a job. It's three months since she worked on the streets. She doesn't want to go back again.

Use CAFOD's magazine for schools, *fairground*, or visit its website. Find out six facts about a current CAFOD project and produce your own fact sheet about it. Use your design or ICT skills and include: where it is; what it does; who it helps; and what kind of help CAFOD needs to continue to support the work.

Thought stop

Helen Keller was blind and deaf but she wrote: 'The greatest calamity that can befall a person is to have sight and yet fail to see... I have walked with people whose eyes are full of light, but who see nothing in wood, sea or sky, nothing in the city streets, nothing in books. They have the sunset, the morning skies, the purple of distant hills, yet their souls voyage through this enchanted world with a barren stare.'

Making connections

Christ has no body on earth now but ours:
no hands but ours, no feet but ours.
Ours are the eyes through which Christ's compassion
is to look upon the world.
Ours are the feet with which he is to go about doing good.
Ours are the hands with which he is to bless others now.

St Teresa of Avila, Spanish Carmelite nun, 1515–1582

Good news

God loved the world so much that he gave his only Son, so that everyone who believes in him may not die but have eternal life.

(John 3:16)

Words of faith

Come back to me with all your heart.
Don't let fear keep us apart.
Trees do bend though straight and tall;
  so must we to others call.

Chorus
Long have I waited for your coming
  home to me
and living deeply our new life.
The wilderness will lead you to your
  heart
where I will speak.

Integrity and justice with tenderness
  you shall know.
You shall sleep secure with peace;
faithfulness shall be your joy.

Weston Priory, Gregory Norbert OSB

Who is the speaker? Do you think this is a good Lenten message? Explain why.

Pressure point

Thought stop

Mark's gospel ends with Jesus' command to his disciples: Go throughout the whole world and tell everyone the good news. The Church continues Jesus' work.

Testing times ❓

1. Give two examples of needs and wants that human efforts cannot meet.

2. What does the name 'Jesus' mean?

3. Name two ways in which Jesus' mission is good news.

4. What celebration marks the beginning of Lent?

5. Name two ways in which Christians mark Lent.

Key *words*

For your Fact File:

Jesus	saviour	salvation
mission	Lent	fasting
justice	almsgiving	

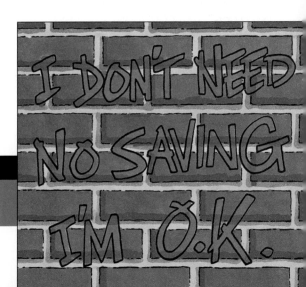

Celebrating Easter

For the sake of Jo

In this section of our work we will be learning:

◆ how people give themselves for others
◆ that at Easter the Church celebrates the death and resurrection of Jesus.

Jo brought home the County Individual Gold Medal. The Spriggs family celebrated.

'All those early morning drives to Loughborough to the Olympic-sized pool,' said Dad, 'it was worth it!'

'Thank goodness for my overtime,' said Mum.

'You were brill!' said Robert. 'I don't mind waiting for my computer upgrade.'

'Look a bit more pleased,' said Julie. 'You won!'

'I am pleased,' Jo said. 'It's just that Miss Foster said I should begin training for the UK trials and I don't know if we can afford that.'

'Now,' said Mum, 'let's have our celebration meal first and then we can talk about how we will afford it.'

1. How have the family helped Jo?
2. Role play the family's discussion. What will they do to help Jo to go on training?

Work as a class

1 ◆ Talk about the story and photographs.
2 ◆ In what ways do people give their lives for others?
3 ◆ Share your thoughts about people who have given themselves for you.
4 ◆ How have you given yourself for others?

Using the title *Whatever the cost*, write a story or poem, produce a piece of artwork or find a picture or photograph that fits the title.

Let's find out about celebrating Easter

The earliest proclamation of the gospel in the New Testament is the good news that 'Christ died for our sins according to the scriptures, was buried and was raised to life on the third day according to the Scriptures'. (1 Corinthians 15:1–5). At Easter the final actions of Jesus' self-sacrifice are celebrated in a special week of liturgies. It is called Holy Week, and the last three days are called the Easter *Triduum*.

triduum: three days

Map the week

1. Match the day and the event in the life of Jesus.
2. Put them in order.

Good Friday	Jesus shares his last supper with his friends
Easter Sunday	Jesus enters Jerusalem; crowds welcome him
Holy Saturday	mocking crowds call for his death; Jesus is crucified
Passion Sunday	Jesus is buried; his friends are devastated
Holy Thursday	the women are messengers of Good News; Jesus is risen

Work as a class

Look at the picture and words that tell the story of the Easter Triduum. For each day identify the celebration, the symbols and prayers used, and what the day means for the Church.

Passion Sunday

Passion Sunday marks the beginning of Holy Week. It is also called Palm Sunday. The Church acts out Jesus' entry into Jerusalem. Crowds of people greet him. He comes to complete his mission.

During Mass the dramatic story of the Passion of Jesus is proclaimed. Everyone takes part. A narrator tells the story. The priest speaks the words of Jesus. A reader takes other speaking parts. All the people speak the words of the crowd.

Blessed is he who comes in the name of the Lord.

Holy Thursday

The Church remembers how Jesus gives himself to his enemies to die on the cross and how Jesus gives himself in bread and wine to his disciples and to the Church forever.

Do this in memory of me.

People keep watch, honouring Jesus present in the Blessed Sacrament and remembering his words: 'Could you not watch an hour with me?' (Matthew 26:40)

Kim's story

Father Eric was saying, 'The washing of feet tonight reminds us that we have to follow the example of Jesus. I'd like each of you to think about the service you give to our parish family. Everyone's service is different. Everyone's is important. I'm going to ask twelve people to come and sit here on the chairs at the front. It will be a sign that you, in your turn, are ready to serve as Jesus did. You will represent the whole parish family.'

The church was quiet when Father Eric finished. Then people started to go up to the front.

'Can I go, Mum?', I whispered; 'I want to go on being an altar server.'

'If you really want to,' said Mum.

So I did.

Father Eric knelt in front of each person. He held one of their feet over a bowl and poured water from a jug. Then he dried it with a towel. Mr Martin from the choir was next to me.

I watched what he did. Then it was my turn. The water was warm. It was all over very quickly.

Father Eric was back at the altar. 'Now,' he said, 'we will do what Jesus did when he gave himself to his disciples in bread and wine. We offer God bread and wine and it will become the Body and Blood of Jesus, given for us.'

Then the Mass continued.

After Mass Father Eric carried the consecrated hosts to the Blessed Sacrament chapel in a procession with candles and incense.

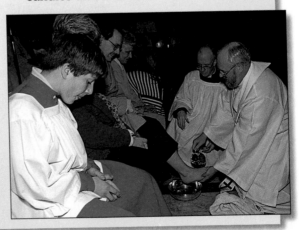

2B Celebrating Easter

Good Friday

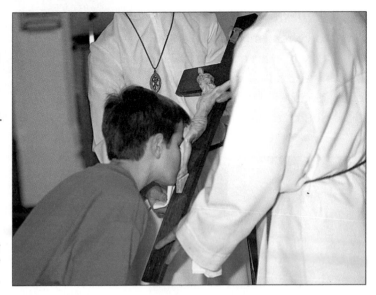

The Church remembers: Jesus is obedient to his Father even to accepting his death. He is crucified and dies on the cross.

Again the dramatic story of the Passion of Jesus is proclaimed with everyone taking part.

This is the wood of the cross on which hung the Saviour of the world.

Chris's story

Yesterday I spent two hours in church, first at a practice for the altar servers and then for the Good Friday liturgy.

The church looked different. The altar was bare and the tabernacle door was wide open so you could see it was empty. There were no flowers and no music when we walked into church in procession. Father Bernard lay face down on the floor and everyone knelt down. It was so quiet.

Then came the reading of the Gospel. Uncle Bob was one of the narrators. All of us took the part of the crowd. It felt strange to say 'Crucify him! Crucify him!'

Then there were a lot of prayers. I'd never thought of praying for people who don't believe in God.

For the Veneration of the Cross, Phil Chu was my partner. We carried the candles. Father Bernard carried a cross covered with a purple cloth. Three times he stopped. Each time he uncovered a bit of the cross and he sang 'This is the wood of the cross on which hung the Saviour of the world'. Everyone answered 'Come, let us adore!' Phil and I had to hold

the cross and everyone came up and kissed the feet of the figure of Jesus. We each had a cloth to wipe the feet of the cross after each person kissed them. Afterwards we helped Father Bernard to put the cross on the wall behind the empty tabernacle. Next, although it was not Mass, people received Holy Communion. Father Bernard brought the consecrated hosts from the Blessed Sacrament chapel.

It was the first time I was an altar server on Good Friday.

Thought stop

Why do Christians hold street processions on Good Friday?

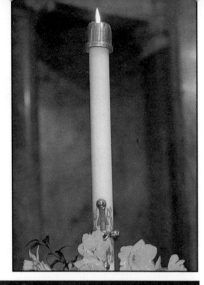

Easter Vigil

The Church celebrates Jesus, risen to new life.

The priest traces the sign of the cross on the Easter candle and adds the numbers of the year and symbols of the wounds of Jesus.

Christ yesterday and today, the beginning and the end,
Alpha and Omega;
all time belongs to him,
and all the ages;
to him be glory and power,
through every age for ever. Amen.
By his holy and glorious wounds may Christ
our Lord guard us and keep us. Amen.

The candle is lit from the new fire. There is a procession into the church. Just as the cross was greeted three times on Good Friday, the Easter candle is greeted three times. The priest or deacon sings 'Christ our Light'. Everyone answers 'Thanks be to God.' Everyone stands with lighted candles for the Easter song of praise called the 'Exultet'. Christ the Light is risen!

Make this new fire holy and inflame us with new hope.

Glory to God! Alleluia!
The song of praise *Glory to God* and the *Alleluia* are sung again. They have not been used during Lent.

Adults who have been preparing for initiation into the Church receive the sacraments of Baptism, Confirmation and the Eucharist.

Thought stop

God so loved the world that he gave his only Son so that all who believe in him may have eternal life.

Classwork

A. Holy Week calendar

Design and make your own Holy Week calendar. Include the order of events, main names and one symbol for each day.

B. Easter Triduum

Choose one day of the Easter Triduum. Write about the signs, symbols and rituals and what they mean.

C. Tell the Easter story

Imagine you have a Hindu friend. Write a letter to tell her about what Christians celebrate at Easter and some of the ways they do this.

Homework

Choose one day of Holy Week and interview someone who has celebrated it. Find out how they took part, what they remember and what they liked about the celebration. Write out the conclusions you have come to from your interview.

Making connections

B 2

≡ Testing times ❓ ≡

1. What does the Church celebrate at Easter?

2. When does the celebration of Easter begin?

3. What is the special name for the last three days of Holy Week?

4. List the events of Holy Week in order.

5. Name two symbols used during the Easter Triduum.

Pressure point

'The night is darkest just before the dawn.'
What other images might give the Easter message of resurrection?

Key words

For your Fact File:

Easter
Triduum
Passion Sunday
Holy Thursday
Good Friday
Holy Saturday
the Easter Vigil
Easter candle
resurrection

Words of faith

This is the day that the Lord has made,
We will rejoice and be glad in it.

This is the day when he rose again...
We will rejoice and be glad in it.

author unknown

What other resurrection songs are used in your school liturgies and worship?

Use your work from this section to try writing a new one for your class or year group.

Tell the Good News

Design an A4 poster that could be displayed in the windows of homes and shops. Include something of the sorrow of Good Friday as well as the joy of Easter Sunday.

Thought stop

Christ has died.
Christ is risen.
Christ will come again

Living as Easter people

Test your memory

Draw and decorate the Easter Candle. (To check your work, see p. 51.)

Underneath, add one word that you think sums up the message of Easter.

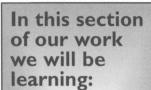

In this section of our work we will be learning:

◆ about the power of light as a symbol of life and hope
◆ about the Church's role as witness to the resurrection of Jesus and the Easter call to new life.

Christ our light

The Church's Easter Vigil begins with the blessing and lighting of the Easter candle.

The candle is a symbol of Jesus, risen to new life, bringing light and hope.

It is a sign that the light of Jesus is for everyone.

It is a sign that Christians are called to walk as 'children of the light'.

Look back to the words that are said to parents and godparents at a Baptism on p. 32.
What are they asked to do?

The Easter Vigil is the time when new adult Christians are baptised. It is also the time when all Christians renew the promises of baptism.
As a class, read the baptismal promises.

Priest: Do you reject sin, so as to live in the freedom of God's children?   **All:** I do.

Priest: Do you reject the glamour of evil, and refuse to be mastered by sin?   **All:** I do.

Priest: Do you reject Satan, father of sin and prince of darkness?   **All:** I do.

Priest: Do you believe in God, the Father almighty, creator of heaven and earth?   **All:** I do.

Priest: Do you believe in Jesus Christ, his only Son, our Lord, who was born of the Virgin Mary, was crucified, died, and was buried, rose from the dead, and is now seated at the right hand of the Father?   **All:** I do.

Priest: Do you believe in the Holy Spirit, the holy catholic Church, the communion of saints, the forgiveness of sins, the resurrection of the body and life everlasting?   **All:** I do.

Think and talk

With a partner, look again at the words from the baptism rite. What do the promises of baptism say about walking in the light and rejecting darkness? Share your ideas with the class.

On this day

Using local and national newspapers for one date, collect examples of:
some of the darkness and evil in the world
people who bring light.

Witnesses

From the beginning the Christian community understood that every member is a witness to the resurrection of Jesus. The way they set about doing this shows they believed he was alive and were confident that they shared the power of his new life.

Paul's story

I was a student of religion in Jerusalem when the Christian community began. I was there when the deacon Stephen was arrested and sentenced to death for saying Jesus was the Saviour sent by God. I watched him being stoned to death; in fact, I looked after the coats of the men who stoned him. Then, as you know, I became an apostle.* Being a witness for Jesus isn't the world's easiest job! I've been thrown out of cities and into prison. I've been whipped, stoned, shipwrecked, sworn at and persecuted. Once I only escaped when my friends lowered me over the city wall in a basket. I've been hungry and thirsty, homeless and sick. But this is nothing when I think of the privilege of knowing Jesus. I am happy to lose everything if I can know Jesus Christ as my Lord and spread his gospel.

Peter's story

It took a while for us to understand what the resurrection of Jesus meant. We found ourselves able to speak and act with confidence. We knew the power we had came from Jesus. Once, John and I were going to the temple for the afternoon prayer. As we came near the Beautiful Gate we met a lame man. He called out to us, 'Spare some change!' I said, 'I have no money, but I give you what I have. In the name of Jesus Christ of Nazareth I order you to get up and walk!' I put out my hand to him and he stood up. The strength came back to his feet and ankles and he began to walk. Then he began to jump and to shout out praising God.

Many people recognised him. They couldn't believe that he was walking. I spoke to them. 'This isn't some power I have. This is God's power revealed in Jesus. We are his witnesses.'

* Look back to 1C, p. 24.

Mary's story

I'll never forget the way Jesus welcomed me. It meant I could leave the past behind and start again. When he was crucified it seemed like the end of the world. We had to hurry to bury him because it was the Sabbath. The Jewish holy day begins on Friday evening and goes on to Saturday evening, so it wasn't until the third day, Sunday morning, that we could go to the tomb. There were three of us, Mary and Salome and me. We took spices to anoint his body. When we got there we saw

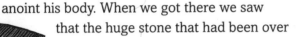

that the huge stone that had been over the entrance to the tomb had been moved. We were shocked and afraid. The others left. I wandered through the garden in tears. I saw someone. I thought it was a gardener and I said, 'If you have taken him away, please tell me where to go and I will take his body away.' The man said, 'Mary?' I looked up. It was Jesus! Can you imagine how I felt?

He asked me to go and tell Peter and the others that he had risen. I did, but they wouldn't believe me, until they had seen him themselves. After that they wanted to tell the whole world.

Classwork ✎

Challenge to new life

A. *Choose one of the witnesses who told their stories. Create a storyboard for a six-frame animated cartoon story. Suggest a title.*

B. *Read more about one of the characters:*

- *what happened to Peter and John (Acts 5:12–21)*

- *how Paul preached the good news to a prison guard (Acts 16:22–39)*

- *when Mary became a disciple (Luke 7:36-50)*

Imagine you are a journalist for the Jerusalem Daily News sent to interview your character. Write your article for the paper. Add an eye-catching headline.

C. *Choose another one of the witnesses who told their stories. What qualities do you think made this person a good witness for the resurrection of Jesus? What qualities do you think a witness needs for the twenty-first century?*

2C Living as Easter people

Witnesses today ...

Christians continue to witness to their faith in Jesus risen and alive.

Homework 🏛

Read Matthew 5:13–16.

Imagine a world without salt. Imagine a world without light.

Write your own one-minute 'Thought for the day' about 'A world without salt' or 'A world without light'.

Making the witness real

CAFOD encourages Catholics to be light and salt in very practical ways. Every time you visit your local supermarket, you enter into trade with the rest of the world. How do you know if it's fair? How do you know if the people who actually produce the things we buy are getting a fair deal? You are an important customer to supermarkets. You have a right to ask: Who is making the profit? Who is paying the price?

Banana Split is a CAFOD Learning Game to help you think about situations of injustice. *Copymaster* 12

Work as a class

Prepare and share a Year 7 assembly on witnesses.

Making connections

Thought stop

Because Jesus is risen…

… there are Catholic schools   …CAFOD works for justice

… the cross is a sign of hope   …Christians can sing 'Alleluia'

… Christmas is celebrated all over the world

Add your own ideas.

Testing times ?

1. Explain the symbolism of the Easter candle.

2. Identify two issues in the world that need the light of Christ.

3. Name one of the first witnesses to the resurrection of Jesus.

4. Christians are called to be salt for the earth and light for the world. Explain what this means.

5. What is CAFOD?

Key words

For your Fact File:

baptismal promises
resurrection
witness
justice

Words of faith

'We are an Easter people and Alleluia is our song!'
Is this a good description for Christians?

Thought stop

In the world today two billion people believe that Jesus is risen. Of these about 1,000,000,000 (one thousand million) are Roman Catholics.

2D Called to change

People can only grow if they are prepared to change the way they think and act. Sometimes this means admitting they are wrong and saying sorry.

Police Chief admits: We got it wrong

Hospital refuses to admit responsibility

Ex POWs say: We'll never forgive

Footballer apologises for spitting

1. Look at the headlines.
2. Who is saying sorry? For what?
3. Choose one headline to write about.

Explain what changes are happening, or might happen, because people say sorry.
4. What happens if people refuse to say sorry?

The power of forgiveness

This is a story about two friends.

Rob was feeling very nervous. He had heard that Bill was back. It would be the first time he had met Bill since the day of the trouble. He thought about how he had run away from the bullies. He remembered how Bill had looked after he had been beaten up.

'What am I going to say?' thought Rob. 'What is he going to say? Will he want to be my friend any more?'

Bill came along the path. He waved. As he came nearer, Rob could see he was smiling. 'Hi!' said Bill. 'You OK?'

Rob didn't know what to say. Bill was acting as if Rob had never let him down.

'We're mates, aren't we?' asked Bill.

'Of, course,' said Rob.

'Good,' said Bill, 'I need to catch up on my work. You'll help, won't you?'

'Sure,' said Rob.

'Because we're mates, aren't we?' asked Bill.

'Of course,' said Rob. And he thought to himself, 'What a friend!'

Think and talk

How is forgiveness important for Rob?
How is forgiveness important for Bill?
What does the story show about the power of forgiveness?

Check Out What You Know ✓
Brainstorm 'Confession'.

Forgiveness: a new beginning

Forgiveness involves at least two people and often, if not always,
leads to new beginnings.

Let's look at a story from the New Testament.
Use the information about the characters to role play the stories.

The characters

Philemon is a leading Christian.
Onesimus is a slave belonging to Philemon.
Paul is the reconciler.

What happened next

The New Testament does not tell us what
happened when Onesimus got back. Either
continue the role play, or write a letter from
Philemon or Onesimus to Paul.

Paul hoped Philemon would forgive
Onesimus and welcome him back because
both were Christians. Both knew the prayer
of the disciples of Jesus: 'Forgive us our
trespasses as we forgive those who trespass
against us.'

The situation

Onesimus runs away.
For a slave to run away is illegal.
Onesimus meets Paul and becomes a Christian.
Paul says Onesimus must go back to his master.
Onesimus doesn't want to because he is afraid.
Paul says he will write a letter to his master,
Philemon. Paul asks Philemon
to receive Onesimus back,
not as a slave, but as
a brother.

It can be easy to say sorry. It may mean:
'Sorry I was caught!' or 'Sorry, I'll avoid
trouble!' What is really hard is to say 'Sorry,
what I did was wrong.' The last kind of sorry
means 'I see the need for a change of heart
and also changes in the way I live.'

Words we use

conversion – change, for example an
attic space into a loft room;
– from one religion to another;
– change that is sorrow for sin, for
example turning back to God and away
from sin

repentance – a change of heart, for
example expressing regret for
wrongdoing;

– a change of behaviour, such as giving
back stolen property

to forgive – to pardon, to start again

to reconcile – to make friends again
to heal a situation and move on after a
quarrel, away from hate, injustice

conscience – the 'inner voice' that helps a
person to make judgements about what
is right and wrong

Celebrating love and mercy

2

The Sacrament of Reconciliation brings the gift of forgiveness and the *grace* to change. It is also called Confession. One of Jesus' most famous stories can help us to understand this Sacrament. The pictures tell the story. (Luke 15:11–32) Match the pictures with the stages of the celebration of the sacrament.

The prodigal father and son

prodigal: generous, free, easy and wasteful
grace: the touch of God's love in our lives

A person puts his or her own wishes before any rule or law of God.

What makes a person have a change of heart?

Examination of conscience

Catholics get ready to celebrate reconciliation by an examination of conscience. They ask themselves 'In what ways have I turned away from God's love and God's ways?'

The priest acting for Jesus and the Church welcomes the returning sinner and invites him or her to confess and to pray an act of contrition.

Act of contrition
Loving God, because of your love and goodness I am sorry for my sins. Help me to turn away from sin. Help me to forgive others as you forgive me. Amen.

The priest speaks the words of forgiveness in the name of Jesus. He welcomes the penitent back to the family of the Church.

The words of forgiveness

God the Father of mercies,
through the death and resurrection of his Son,
has reconciled the world to himself and sent
the Holy Spirit among us for the forgiveness of sins;
through the ministry of the Church
may God give you pardon and peace,
and I absolve you from your sins in the name of
the Father and of the Son and of the Holy Spirit.

Penitents are asked to do something to show that their sorrow is real. This is called a penance. It is a sign of willingness to change.

2D Called to change

Talk about …

The story

What was the younger son's attitude before and after his return? What was the father's attitude? Why was the older brother angry? Who sinned? Who forgave? How did all the characters in the story have to change?

The Sacrament

What makes people want to say sorry? How is this sacrament a celebration? Name some selfish attitudes which lead to selfish actions that might be confessed, for example, greed leads to stealing.

What are some of the consequences of sins? Does everyone have a conscience? Suggest three questions that would help someone to examine his or her conscience.

Classwork

A. Use your Bible skills

Find Psalm 50. Choose some words from the psalm about God's love, mercy and forgiveness. Write them into your book and say why you have chosen them.

B. The story goes on...

Write a short story that begins: 'The next morning…' In your story either tell how the younger son showed that his repentance was real; or what the elder son did.

C. Steps to change

Look back to the story of the prodigal son. Explain what had to happen before the son could receive his father's love and mercy. What does the Church say are the steps a person must take if he or she is to celebrate the Sacrament of Reconciliation?

What's in a name?

The Sacrament of Reconciliation has two other names: the Sacrament of Penance and the Sacrament of Confession. How do these different names help people to understand what the sacrament is about?

Homework

Write three sentences to show what you have learned about the Sacrament of Reconciliation. What do the different names say about what the sacrament offers Christians?

Extra!

Invite a priest to come and talk with your class about the Sacrament of Reconciliation.

Making connections

Testing times ?

1. Why was Paul confident that Philemon would forgive Onesimus?

2. How does the story of the prodigal son show sorrow, forgiveness and reconciliation?

3. What are the four stages of the Sacrament of Reconciliation?

4. What does 'to examine your conscience' mean?

5. What does 'contrition' mean?

Thought stop

Christians aren't perfect, just forgiven.

Good news

Jesus said: There is more happiness in heaven over one sinner who repents than over ninety-nine people who do not need to repent. (Luke 15:7)

Pressure point

'I can say sorry to God anytime. I don't need a sacrament.'

Key words

For your Fact File:

conversion
repentance
forgiveness
reconciliation
penance
confession
change of heart
conscience
contrition

What's your view?

Two artists' paintings of the prodigal son: what do you see? What would you paint?

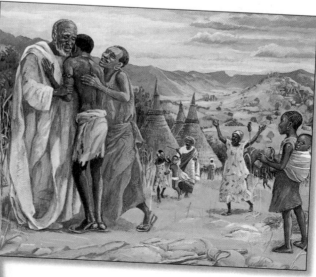

2D Called to change

A place for prayer

Every part of a human person grows. People grow physically. They also grow in their emotions, their minds and their spirit.

There's more to me than meets the eye

If an adult human body was analysed, we would discover that it is made of:

about 45 litres of water
enough carbon to make the lead of 9,000 pencils
enough phosphorus for the heads of 2,000 matches
enough iron to make a nail
about 30 grams of other metals
enough fat to make about 8 bars of soap
enough sulphur to rid a dog of fleas
enough lime to whitewash a small shed

If this was the only description of you, what would be missing?

Use words from the Wordstore to help you to write your answer. Add some words of your own.

In this section of our work we will be learning:

◆ about the spiritual side of being human
◆ that the Our Father is the model of Christan prayer, and some Catholic prayer traditions.

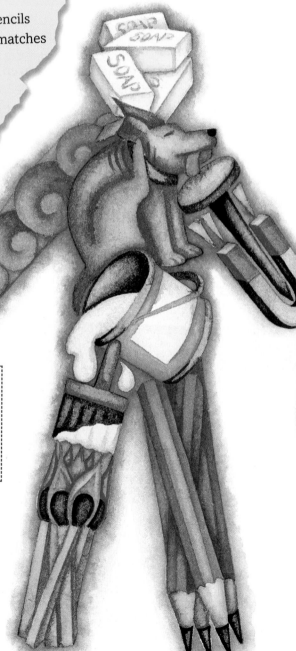

Wordstore

individual	feelings
talents	friendships
relationships	history
humour	personality
smile	laughter

Think and talk
Use your Bible skills to find Psalm 8.
How does the psalmist express the wonder of being human?

Prayer

People everywhere recognise one activity as part of the
spiritual side of the human person. This activity is prayer.

Check out what you know ✓

In groups, brainstorm 'prayer'. Share your ideas with the
class.

Work as a class

Look at the pictures and decide:

Who is praying? Where? How?

What does this tell you about the place of prayer in human life?

What does this tell you about the spiritual side of humans?

From the work you have done, write two sentences to
explain in your own words what prayer is and why it is
important for people.

The prayer of all disciples

One day the disciples asked Jesus, 'Lord, teach us to pray.'
The prayer Jesus taught them is the Our Father. It is also
called the Lord's Prayer. It is the model for all Christian
prayer. All Christians share this prayer.

Read the different versions of the prayer.

Our Father, who art in heaven,
hallowed be thy name:
thy kingdom come;
thy will be done on earth as it is in heaven.
Give us this day our daily bread,
and forgive us our trespasses
as we forgive those who trespass against us,
and lead us not into temptation,
but deliver us from evil.
Amen (The Sunday Missal)

Our Father in heaven,
hallowed be your name;
your kingdom come,
your will be done
on earth as in heaven.
Give us today our daily bread.
Forgive us our sins
as we forgive those
who sin against us.
Lead us not into temptation
but deliver us from evil.
For the kingdom, the power
and the glory are yours
now and for ever.
Amen (The Alternative Service Book 1980)

Our Father in heaven,
hallowed be your name,
your kingdom come,
your will be done
on earth as in heaven.
Give us today our daily bread.
Forgive us our sins
as we forgive those who sin against us.
Save us from the time of trial
and deliver us from evil.
Amen (A new version)

Think and talk

1. What does the prayer tell us about God?
   About Jesus? About the disciples?
2. In what ways can calling God 'Father' help
   Christians to pray?
3. What links can you make between the
   words of the Our Father and work you
   have done this year about:
   – Jesus and his mission
   – the call to be a disciple
   – the Sacrament of Reconciliation.

Thought stop

'**Our** Father' = '**Our** family'

Words we use

hallow – to praise God; to make holy
by blessing

kingdom – God's rule, God's presence

Classwork

A. The Our Father can be divided into two parts, one about God and one about people. In your own words explain (a) What does it say about God? (b) What does it say about people?

B. If all the world were to pray the Our Father, what difference would it make to the young, the old, men, women, children, the poor, the rich, the homeless, the sad, the lonely? Choose four of these different kinds of people to write about.

C. Use the words of the reflection on the Our Father (p.69) to make lists under two headings: 'Christian privileges' and 'Christian responsibilities'.

1. Read Matthew 6:5–8 and Matthew 7:7–11.

2. What have you learned about prayer from these passages that you did not know?

The Prayer of the Church

As a faithful Jew, Jesus would have learned the psalms of his people. The Book of Psalms in the Old Testament is a collection of 150 of these prayer songs. It is a prayer book and history book in one. The psalms recall all the reasons the People of Israel have to praise God. They also recall the bad times when God seemed to be asleep. 'Wake up, God!' says Psalm 44:23

Think and talk

Use your Bible skills to find:
Psalm 22: How does it picture God?
Psalm 134: When would people pray this?
Psalm 43: How is the writer feeling?

The psalms have always been part of the prayer of the Church. About six hundred years after the time of Jesus a young man called Benedict began to live a hermit's life in central Italy. Others saw how he lived and prayed and asked to join him. They lived, worked and prayed together. They were called monks, and the places where they lived were monasteries. Benedict's sister, Scholastica, began a monastery for women. They were called nuns.

The Prayer of the Church grew out of the life of the monastery. The monks and nuns prayed eight times a day. They would sing the psalms. They developed a special music for this called plainsong, or Gregorian chant. They listened to readings from Scripture and the writings of saints of the Church. They prayed for everyone in need.

In groups: *Copymaster* [13]

The life of Jesus in prayer

The rosary is the life of Jesus in a special prayer. People pray the rosary to help them to remember and think prayerfully about the main events in Jesus' life. Jesus' mother, Mary, knew him better than any other person. Luke's gospel tells us that she 'treasured in her heart' what Jesus said and did. The rosary prayer helps people to do this like Mary and with her help.

Homework

The prayer of the Church: Copymaster [14]

2E A place for prayer

Making connections

Tips for prayer

Use the work you have done in this section to suggest two tips for prayer. Make a poster or bookmark using one or both of your tips.

Key words

∙ ∙

For your Fact File:

prayer
spiritual
meditation
Our Father
Prayer of the Church
rosary

Prayer time

Plan and use a 15 minute prayer or reflection time for the class. Remember that perhaps not everyone will want to join in vocal prayer, so include time for quiet reflection. Think carefully about the symbols and music you might use to help everyone to take part in some way.

Pressure point

'My prayers are not answered, so why should I bother?'

Words of faith

Receive my prayer as incense,
my uplifted hands as an evening sacrifice.

These words are from Psalm 141. Why is incense used in worship and as a symbol of prayer?

Testing times ?

1. Explain what prayer is in your own words.

2. What is the prayer that is common to all Christians? What words of the prayer express this?

3. From the Our Father choose two Christian beliefs about God and two rules for Christian living.

4. What is the Prayer of the Church?

5. Name three mysteries of the rosary.

The prayer for all times and places: Our God

Our God, who art in heaven, hallowed be your name in peoples across the world, of different races, colours and religions; single people; couples and families; people at work or out of work, at home or homeless.

May your Kingdom come and your will be done on earth, in the ways in which we act, the choices we make, the action for change which we take and which we encourage in others.

Give us this day our daily bread: which we work for, food which we share, bread which no one should be denied because of the greed of others.

Forgive us our trespasses: times when we have condemned instead of being constructive; times when we have not listened but only preached; times when we have failed to do what we know we should have done; times when we have not shown compassion and forgiveness.

Lead us not into temptation: temptation to close our minds, our ears and our eyes to reality; temptation to be afraid to speak out against injustice; temptation to think it's all too much and that what we do won't make any difference; temptation to think that there is no alternative.

Deliver us from evil: the evil of a world where people don't count; the evil of powerlessness and loss of hope; the evil of a world where gates, walls and barriers between people grow even higher; the evil of a world where money is more important than people and where the last debt repayment must be squeezed out of developing countries.

May your kingdom come, for yours is the kingdom, the power and the glory for ever and ever. Amen.

From Celebrating One World, *a workshop resource on social justice, edited by Linda Jones (CAFOD) and Annabel Shilson-Thomas, p.143.*

2E A place for prayer

Other faiths: Hinduism

We are going to learn about and reflect on some things about the Hindu religion. Next year we will be learning about Judaism, and in Year 9 we will learn about Islam.

Check out what you know ✓

There are many different religious traditions in Britain. These figures are for people who have some association with the faith in question. They are not necessarily active members. (Figures from *Religions in the UK*, a multi-faith directory, 1998.)

Buddhists	30,000+
Muslims	1,000,000
Sikhs	350,000+
Hindus	400,000+
Jews	300,000
Christians	40,000,000

> ### In this section of our work we will be learning:
>
> ◆ about the Hindu religion and where Hindu communities are in Britain
> ◆ about Hindu belief in Brahman, the Supreme Being.

1. With a partner, share which of these faith communities you have heard of.
2. Do you know anyone who belongs to that faith? Think of family, friends, neighbours, pop stars and athletes.
3. Do a bar chart showing the range of membership of the different faith communities in Britain.
4. What does this tell you about Britain?

Look at this map. India is where the Hindu tradition began. Hindus in Britain have migrated mainly from India and East Africa, and also from other parts of the world: Uganda, Zambia and Kenya. There are over 800,000,000 Hindus in the world. There have been Hindus in Britain for hundreds of years. The largest Hindu communities in Britain are in Greater London, Birmingham, Coventry and Leicester. There are around 161 Hindu places of worship in Britain.

1. On the map, identify the countries named.
2. On a map of Britain, find the places where large Hindu communities live.

Thought stop

Britain is a multi-faith country.

In your work this year you have been learning about communities. Not only do you belong to the community of your family, neighbourhood and school, but you may also belong to the community of all those who have religious faith.

The Catholic Church believes that all peoples form one community, because God is the creator of all human life. Each human person is created to share God's life and so the Church recognises and respects the search for God of other religions and faith communities.

Learn about a Hindu believer

'My name is Indira Shah. I was born in Coventry where I live with my family. There is my dad, Anand; my mum, Chandra; my brother, Ramon, and my baby sister Rivka. I have family who live in India, my aunts, uncles and cousins. We are saving up to visit them.

I have just started at a big secondary school. I am hoping to make lots of new friends. So far the lessons I like best are drama, English, science and RE.

As well as ordinary school, I also go to special language classes. These are to teach me to read Sanskrit, the sacred language in which our Hindu scriptures are written.

'Aum' or 'Om' is the most sacred symbol and sound in Hinduism. It is believed to be the first sound of creation. It is spoken before reading the Hindu scriptures, prayer or medicine.

Some other important words in Hinduism are:

Itihasa	Rig Veda	Vedas
a holy book which contains Hindu stories	the most sacred of the Hindu holy books	the oldest of the Hindu holy books

These sacred books tell us about the Supreme God, Brahman, and how many male and female gods express some form or aspect of Brahman. They watch over, protect and care for the earth and all people. These stories are symbolic. They describe, in colourful ways, the power and majesty of God and the way in which God controls the earth. At many Hindu festivals these stories are told and acted out and brought to life again.'

Homework 🏛

Mahatma Gandhi (1869–1948) is a major leader for Hindus. Find out all you can about him, how he lived and what he taught.
Is his message still important today or not, and why?
Write up your findings in an interview format.

Hindu belief in Brahman

Hinduism is a word that describes many different beliefs and practices. There is no one special founder, no one special scripture, no one special way of doing things. What is important to Hindus is belief in the One Supreme, Brahman. The One Supreme can be pictured, understood and spoken about in many different ways. In the Hindu scriptures is written: 'God is One, but the wise call it by many names.'

The images of God take on special shapes, forms and qualities and have special names.

Ganesha is the symbol of good fortune.

Shiva is the dancer and destroyer.

Saraswati is the goddess of learning.

Lakshmi is the goddess of good fortune.

Indira

'The image of God that I find most helpful is Saraswati, the goddess of learning. I pray to her just before exams!'

Ramon

'The image of God that I like best is Hanuman. He represents strength and loyalty, the qualities I want to have.'

Think and talk

Choose one of the Hindu deities pictured above. What do you see?

Thought stop

How important for a person's faith is the way he or she names God?

Classwork

A. With a partner, draw up a list of questions you would need to ask to help you really understand what these pictures of Hindu deities symbolise. Share these with the class. Divide into groups; choose one of the deities and research the answers to the questions.

B. Use the library to find books about Hinduism, an encyclopedia of religions, a video or the Internet site your teacher suggests. Choose one Hindu deity and see what stories you can find. Bring your findings to the class.

C. What do these images tell you about Hindu belief in the One Supreme?

Making connections

Words of faith

> You can live for a few days without eating, but not without praying. Prayer is the key of the morning and the bolt of the evening. Prayer is a sacred alliance between God and the human person.
>
> *Gandhi*

What do these words tell you about Gandhi's faith?

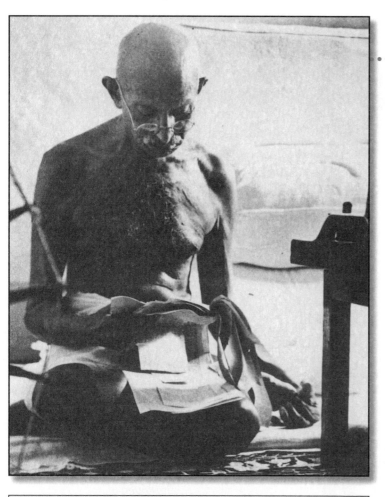

Thought stop

For Hindus, looking at the deities shows them something of Brahman, the Supreme Being, who is beyond all description, and allows Brahman to 'see' them. What does this tell you about the Hindu way of life?

Key words

For your Fact File:

Hinduism
deities
Sanskrit
Brahman
Rig Veda

Using ICT skills, design an overhead that you could use to begin a discussion about Indira and her Hindu faith.

Finally

Why is it important to learn about other faiths?
What have I gained?

Testing times ?

1. *How many Hindus are there in Britain/the world?*
2. *'God is One, but the wise call it by many names.' How does this describe Hinduism?*
3. *Name a Hindu deity that you have learned about.*
4. *Draw the sacred word 'Aum' and explain its meaning.*
5. *What is at the heart of Hindu belief?*

Unit 3 Becoming fully human

In this section of our work we will be learning:

◆ about how we come to know ourselves and what makes a person feel valued
◆ that God is the Giver of Life
◆ that human beings are made in God's image with special privileges and responsibilities.

How well do you know yourself?

1. Draw two circles, one for when you were aged six and one for now.
2. From the Wordstore choose words that best describe you
   (a) when you were six; (b) now.
3. Put the words in the two circles.
4. Share your findings with a partner.
   Was it easier to choose words for now or for when you were six?
   Did your partner agree with the words you have chosen for yourself now?
   Did any of the words your partner chose surprise you?
5. Who do you think knows you best? Why?
6. Who has helped you to know yourself? How did they help?
7. What events have helped you to know yourself?

Wordstore

genuine	purposeful	unique	independent
dependent	special	chatty	individual
noisy	shy	original	exceptional
nervous	tidy	organised	scatty
sporty	untidy	happy	sad
musical	quiet	lazy	artistic

Extra!

'You can't judge a book by its cover.'
'There's more to me than meets the eye.'

1. What do you think these two sayings mean?
2. How do labels or titles affect the way we see people?

74

Think and talk: *People, not labels*

Work in groups. Sometimes people are identified by what they do. Look at this list.

priest	judge
engineer	police officer
school meals attendant	Member of Parliament
bishop	carer
labourer	gardener
caretaker	lawyer
scout leader	deacon
traffic warden	doctor
secretary	mechanic
dentist	teacher
parent	bus driver
street-sweeper	dish-washer

Do these labels tell you anything about the person behind the job they do? Is this all there is to say about them? Which jobs are unpaid?

Choose a teacher to interview

From your work with this teacher, what three interests do you think they have? Work out some questions to help you find out about the person behind the job they do. Make an appointment for your interview. Present your findings to the class.

The real you

It is hard to say what the 'real you' is. The cells of your body are changing and growing all the time. Your physical body is not the same as it was when you were one year old. Is the 'real you' your mind with its memories and knowledge? Is there a difference between the 'you' that others see and the person you know 'inside'? People of many religions believe that human beings are made up of physical bodies and an inner 'spirit' or 'soul'.

Work with a partner

1. Ask your friend to write down four facts about the 'you' she or he knows. Do the same for your friend.
2. Each write down four facts about yourself.
3. Compare what you have written about yourself and what your friend wrote about you.
4. What was the same?
5. What was different?
6. What does this tell you?
7. Share your conclusions with the class.

Check out what you know

'Made in the image of God.' Who is? What does this say to you?

In the beginning

People have always asked questions about themselves and the world. Where do we come from? Why are we here? Where does the world come from? Where is it going?

The authors of the *Book of Genesis* were trying to answer these questions.

Today, the Church still reads their message about God the Creator.

Genesis: beginning

There are two creation accounts in Genesis.

The authors were not present when the world began. They were not scientists. They were trying to express the special relationship of God with his people and God's first gift, life.

They wanted the people to remember the great things that God had done for them. The first account of creation is shaped like a poem. Read Genesis 1 and 2:4.

Look out for the 'days'.

Let there be light!

Let there be a dome to divide the waters!

Let the water below the sky come together and dry land appear! Let the earth produce all kinds of plants!

Let there be lights to separate day from night!

Let the waters be filled with living creatures! Let there be birds in the sky!

Let the earth produce living creatures! Let us make human beings in our own image!

On the seventh day

God rested.
God blessed the
seventh day and
made it holy.

Think and talk

The writers of Genesis were naming all that makes up life.

Work in groups, each taking one day.

Imagine life without each of the following. Think about what each gives to our lives and what it would be like without this.
- day and night (day 1)
- space (day 2)
- earth and water, seed-bearing plants (day 3)
- time and seasons (day 4)
- sea creatures and birds (day 5)
- animals and people (day 6)
- rest and leisure (day 7)

1. What is the writer's message about human beings and what they need?
2. What is the writer's message about creation?
3. What is the writer's message about God?

Today scientists can measure space and chart the history of life on earth. Like the writers of Genesis, scientists are fascinated by the mystery of the universe. One scientist wrote: 'Today it is generally considered that the universe is about 15 billion years old. Being in touch with 15 billion years of activity is mind-boggling!'

Here are two ways to try to imagine the size and age of the universe.

Thought stop

We are God's work of art, created in Christ Jesus to live the good life as from the beginning he had meant us to live it. (Ephesians 2:10)

A space station's way of helping visitors to imagine the scale of the universe.

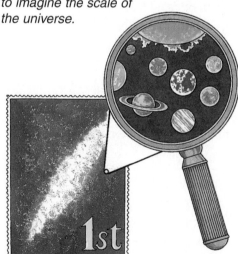

A scientific timeline for creation.

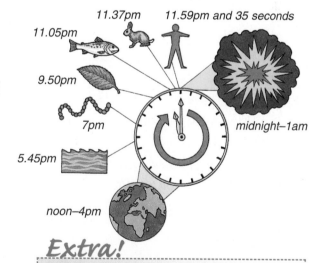

Homework

Draw a diagram to show the seven days of creation. Use words and pictures to explain the Genesis message. Use your ICT skills.

Write one sentence to sum up the Genesis message beginning: 'God is ...'

Extra!

Other Old Testament writers express wonder at God's power in creation with thanks and praise.
Use your Bible skills to find: Psalm 104, Psalm 148, Job 12:7–10.
Choose the verse or verses you like best.
Use your ICT or design skills to make them into a prayer card or poster.

Unique!

The Church believes that life is God's gift. Each person is unique: each has the right to be treated with respect. Each person is created in the image of God and reflects God in a unique way. That is why no one should be denied respect and dignity because of their colour, age, gender or other differences.

The Church believes that the world is God's gift. God trusts people with the care of creation.

The Church believes that God invites each person into a special relationship. The word for this is covenant.

Jewish people today celebrate this covenant on the Sabbath, the seventh day. It is a day of rest, prayer and family celebrations, the holy day of rest that God created.

The Church believes that Jesus makes this covenant 'new' and celebrates it on the first day of the week, Sunday, the day of Jesus' resurrection.

Classwork ✍

A. Over to you

1 *In groups, make two lists to show the privileges and responsibilities human beings have.*

2 *Discuss your lists as a class. Add to your work if you think you have missed something important.*

3 *Make a record of your work using words and illustrations or pictures from magazines.*

B. Naming God

Genesis names God as Creator and Friend. What other ways do people think about God?

1 *Use your Bible skills to find some other images of God from the scriptures: Psalm 18; Jeremiah 18:5–6; Exodus 19:3–6.*

2 *Discuss your answers with a partner. Add any new ideas to your work.*

3 *Use thought bubbles with words and/or pictures to write up your work.*

C. God's way

The prophet Micah summed up the way God's people must live:

'This is what the Lord asks of you: to act justly, to love tenderly, to walk humbly with your God.' (Micah 6:8)

What does this say about the special relationship between God and a human person?

Extra!

Work on your own or in a small group. Write a short radio or TV discussion on human dignity. Make one of the people a Christian.

Include some of the ideas in this section of work. Record or video your discussion, or read it out to the rest of the class.

Making connections

'Creation is God's gift to human beings.'

'Human beings are God's gift to creation.'
Either write a poem or story, *or* design a poster or T-shirt to express one or both of these ideas.

Pass it on

Tell the story of creation in words and pictures for young children.

Words of faith

Have you ever sung the hymn *All Things Bright and Beautiful*? How much can you remember of it? What different images of creation might a modern hymn writer use?

Thought stop

God says:
'I have called you by your name, you are mine.'
What do these words say about God?
What do these words say about how God sees each person?
How might someone feel about themselves after reading them?

Testing times ?

1. What does God say about each day of creation? What does this show?

2. Why is the seventh day so important to Jews and the first day of the week important to Christians?

3. What does the word 'covenant' mean?

4. 'Created in the image of God.' Explain what this means for human beings.

5. Name two ways in which Christians can live out their responsibilities for creation.

Pressure point

'Nowadays everyone knows it took more than seven days to make the world. Genesis is out of date!'

Key *words*

For your Fact File:

unique
creator
creation
self-knowledge
created in the image of God
freedom
dignity
covenant
privilege
responsibility

3A Who am I?

3B Celebrating Pentecost

In this section of our work we will be learning:

◆ about the creative energy and power that everyone has
◆ that God the Holy Spirit is the source of creative energy and saving power.

Test your memory

Think back to the work you did in 3A. Name one key fact you learned about the special role in creation that God gave to human beings.

Alfred's shock

Alfred Nobel got a shock when he opened his newspaper. There was an announcement of his death. Curious, he began to read it. The writer praised his success as a businessman and tried to estimate how much he was worth. He thought that Alfred would be remembered as the man who developed dynamite and gelignite. This shocked Alfred. His skills and training as a chemist had led to the development of a power to blow up the world.

Alfred thought of his brother who had died after an accidental explosion. He thought of dynamite in the wrong hands. There and then he came to a decision. This was not how he wanted to be remembered.

Alfred arranged for money to be made available each year for five Nobel prizes. They are still awarded. Perhaps the most famous of these is the Peace Prize. It means that Alfred's wish to be remembered for something good has come true.

Think and talk

1. What had Alfred's creative skills led him to develop?
2. What was he afraid would happen?
3. One of the Nobel prizes is for Peace. Find out what the others are.
4. Use the library or Internet to find out about one Nobel prize-winner who used his or her creative energy for the good of the world. Write a paragraph about the person and his or her work that could be used in an encyclopedia.

Creative energy and imagination can show themselves in a variety of ways. Everyone has creative energy. Disabilities and difficulties need not prevent people from using it. How do you use your creative energy?

Thought stop

Reach for the stars

Use your imagination

Work in a group and decide:

– the best colour to suggest creative energy at its most powerful and its most gentle…
– the best symbols to suggest creative energy at its most destructive and its most life-giving…
– the best sounds to suggest creative energy at its most wild and most peaceful.

Can you see the wind?

The Church believes that God, the Holy Spirit, is the source of both creative energy and saving power. The Church uses the language of symbols to describe this Holy Spirit.

Look at the language of symbols in the pictures and hymns on this page and the next. If you can, listen to or sing the hymns.

Holy Spirit of fire, flame everlasting, so bright and clear,
Speak this day in our hearts, lighten our darkness and purge us of fear,
Holy Spirit of fire.

Chorus
The wind can blow or be still, or water be parched by the sun,
A fire can die into dust:
But here the eternal Spirit of God tells us a new world's begun.

Holy Spirit of love, strong are the faithful who trust your pow'r.
Love who conquers our will, teach us the words of the gospel of peace,
Holy Spirit of love.

Holy Spirit of Fire. Revd John Glynn

Read Ezekiel 37:1–10.

The Church believes that God the Holy Spirit comes as a gift to the Church at Pentecost. The Church celebrates Pentecost as its 'birthday', its beginning.

A Song from Iona: *Pentecost*

God's Spirit came at Pentecost
To folk who feared their faith was lost;
Inspired by wind and fire of grace,
They faced a market place.

And there, in tongues they'd never known,
They preached the gospel Christ had shown.
Some scorned the depths to which they'd sunk;
Some laughed and called them drunk.

Despite the jeers, amidst the scorn,
The Holy Catholic Church was born,
Fulfilling what the prophets said
And following where Christ led.

The multi-racial audience heard
What God, through the apostles, said;
And many, who had come to mock,
Stayed to believe and talk.

Even now, as in the earliest day,
We feel uncertain. Yet we pray:
Lord, shake and stir your Church again
Till noticed like drunk men.

Thus may the God of all be blessed;
Thus may Christ's gospel be confessed;
Thus may the Spirit where we meet,
Bless sanctuary and street.

From *Wild Goose Songs*, Vol 2, Iona Community

Classwork

A. You are an eye-witness to the events of Pentecost Day. Read Acts 2:1-13. What evidence is there that the apostles were transformed and their lives were changed? Present your evidence as a six-frame story-board.

B. Choose one of the symbols of the Holy Spirit and write a poem or a short paragraph to express what it means.

C. Find the account of Pentecost in the Acts of the Apostles (Acts 2:1–13). Divide a page into two columns with headings: The Pentecost Song (Iona) The Story of Pentecost (Acts). Fill in the words that match the song and the story (events, people, symbols).

Look around you

The Hebrew word for the Spirit is *rûah*. Our nearest English word is 'breath'. When you breathe you take in air, and without air to breathe you would die. Christians believe that the Holy Spirit is as important for living a Christian life as air is for breathing. The Spirit is the gift Jesus promised, the Helper who would enable the disciples and spread his gospel message. It is the power of God the Holy Spirit that *inspires* people and gives life to the Church.

to inspire: breathe in; fill with breath; make creative; fill with life

As evidence of God the Holy Spirit's presence and power, the Church points to gifts and fruits.

Gifts of the Holy Spirit

wisdom
understanding
knowledge
right judgement
courage
reverence
awe and wonder

Fruits of the Holy Spirit

love
joy
peace
patience
kindness
goodness
faithfulness
gentleness
self-control

Work in groups

1 ◆ Read Galatians 5: 22–25 and Isaiah 11: 1–2.
2 ◆ Match the gifts of the Holy Spirit with the fruits they bring.
3 ◆ Share your ideas with the class. Listen to the ideas of others.
4 ◆ Create a class display of gifts and fruits you find in your class, school and families. Use words, photographs and artwork.

Homework

Choose two gifts of the Holy Spirit. Collect and present evidence of the fruits that come from them: at home, at school, in the world.

Use for your sources at least one of the following: a school newspaper or magazine, a Catholic newspaper or magazine, your own memories of events at school, memories of a friend or teacher.

Extra!

Father, Son and Holy Spirit
John's gospel records two promises Jesus made to his disciples about God. Through these Christians learn to know God as Father, Son and Holy Spirit, three persons, the Trinity. Each person is God and the three are One God.
Read John 14:23–26.
How would these promises have encouraged the disciples of Jesus?
How might these promises encourage Christians today?

Thought stop

Young people, the world of today needs you, for it needs men and women who are filled with the Holy Spirit. It needs your courage and hopefulness, your faith and perseverance. The world of tomorrow will be built by you.

Pope John Paul II at Coventry, Pentecost 1982

3B Celebrating Pentecost

Making connections

Thought stop

Stop!
How do Christians today speak about the Holy Spirit? What signs and symbols do they use? Choose a hymn or a prayer to help you.

Think!
Think about someone who is an example of using the gifts of the Holy Spirit to bear fruit.

Go!
Write a short pen-portrait of this person. If you can, include 'interviews' with people who have met the person or been helped by them.

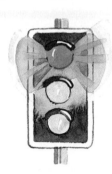

Key words

For your Fact File:

Holy Spirit

Pentecost

creative energy

gifts of the Spirit

fruits of the Spirit

Testing times ?

1. Choose two symbols used to describe the Holy Spirit. What do they say about Christian belief in the Holy Spirit?

2. Which symbol of the Holy Spirit do you find most meaningful? Why?

3. What did Jesus promise about the Holy Spirit?

4. What happened on Pentecost Day?

5. Name two gifts of the Holy Spirit and explain how they might bear fruit in everyday life.

Pressure point

Words of faith

Come Holy Spirit, fill the hearts of your faithful!

Why might this be a risky prayer?

Life shared

Test your memory

A community is…

Name three communities that you belong to.

Name two ways of contributing to a parish community.

(Check your answers from your Fact File and your work on 1A.)

You know what it is like to be part of different communities. A family is a community. A school is a community. A parish is a community.

Ups and downs

As a class, plan a series of short scenes to illustrate the 'ups and downs' of belonging to a community. In groups, improvise the scenes.

Work together

What do your scenes show about how people contribute to the community, or not?

Think and talk

In 1994, the people of South Africa had a new flag. It represents 'The Rainbow People'. It is a sign of hope for a restored nation, a community trying to live in peace.

How does the flag represent new hope for the people of South Africa?

Why was Nelson Mandela a sign of hope for the people of South Africa?

Extra!

Find out about another situation in the world where people are working to build community.

> **In this section of our work we will be learning:**
> ◆ about the demands of building community
> ◆ about the beginnings of the Christian Church
> ◆ about Christian Churches in your neighbourhood.

A parable of community

Read or improvise as a drama script.

Narrator *Once all the colours in the world started to quarrel; each one claimed to be the best, the most important, the most useful and the favourite.*

Green *Clearly I am the most important. I am the sign of life and hope. I was chosen for grass, trees, leaves – without me, all the animals would die. Look out over the countryside and you will see that I am in the majority.*

Blue (interrupting) *You only think about the earth, but consider the sky and the blue sea. It is water that is the basis of life and this is drawn up by the clouds from the blue sea. The sky gives space and peace. Without my peace you would all be nothing but busybodies.*

Yellow (chuckling) *You are all so serious. I bring laughter and warmth into the world. The sun is yellow, the moon is yellow, the stars are yellow. Every time you look at the sunflower, the whole world starts to smile. Without me there would be no fun.*

Red (unable to stay silent, shouting) *I'm the ruler of all! Blood! Life's blood! I am the colour of danger and of bravery. I am willing to fight for a cause. I am the colour of passion and of love.*

Purple (drawing up to his full height, solemnly) *I am the colour of royalty and power. Kings, chiefs and bishops have always chosen me, for I am a sign of authority and wisdom. People do not question me – they listen and obey.*

Indigo (quietly but determinedly) *Think of me. I am the colour of silence. You hardly notice me, but without me you would not see the rest. You need me for balance and contrast, for prayer and inner peace.*

Narrator *The colours went on boasting, each convinced that they were the best. Their quarrelling became louder and louder. Suddenly there was a startling flash of brilliant white lightning; thunder rolled and boomed. Rain started to pour down relentlessly. The colours all crouched in fear, drawing close to one another for comfort.*

Rain *You foolish colours, fighting among yourselves. Do you not know that God made you all? Each unique and different and each for a special purpose. God loves you all. God wants and needs you all. Join hands with one another and come with me.*

Narrator *And God led the colours across the sky in a great bow of colour.*

Rain *Together you will be a reminder of God's love in the world and a sign of hope for tomorrow.*

Narrator *So whenever a rainbow appears in the sky remember: without the uniqueness of each one the whole is incomplete.*

Life together

Community is part of God's plan. Everyone is called to belong. Everyone is called to share in the building of community. The first Christian communities heard about Jesus' new commandment: Love one another. They soon found that building community is costly. It takes time and effort. We learn about the first Christian communities from Luke's book, The Acts of the Apostles.

Work in groups

Read Acts 2:41–47; 4:32–37.

1 ◆ What does this tell you about the first Christian community?
2 ◆ You are a visitor to Jerusalem. What would you want to tell your friends back home about the new community of followers of Jesus?
3 ◆ Write a postcard or letter home.

More Christians, new Churches

Many people spread the Christian message. One of the most famous was St Paul. You have heard how he stopped persecuting Christians and began to spread the gospel. He did not always find it easy.

Classwork

A. Paul in Corinth

Read Acts 18:1–18.

1. What did Paul do in Corinth?
2. Who helped him?
3. Who made difficulties?
4. What did Paul do to sort out the problems?

5. Eyewitness: You were there when Paul came to Corinth. Write a half-column news item for the local paper. Use as the headline either 'We Don't Want Your Sort Here!' or 'Travelling Preacher Thrown Out of Synagogue'.

3C Life shared

After Paul left, the Church at Corinth continued to grow. Like any community, they had their ups and downs. We know about some of these from two of Paul's letters to the Corinthians. One of their quarrels was about who was important. Some Jewish Christians thought they were more important than the Greek Christians because the Jews had been God's chosen people for centuries. This was Paul's reply:

'Christ is like a single body, which has many parts; it is still one body, even though it is made up of different parts. In the same way, all of us, whether Jews or *Gentiles*, whether slaves or free, have been baptised into the one body by the same Spirit, and we have all been given the one Spirit to drink.

For the body itself is not made up of only one part, but of many parts. If the foot were to say, "Because I am not a hand, I don't belong to the body," that would not keep it from being a part of the body. And if the ear were to say, "Because I am not an eye, I don't belong to the body," that would not keep it from being a part of the body. If the whole body were just an eye, how could it hear? And if it were only an ear, how could it smell? … So then, the eye cannot say to the hand, "I don't need you!" Nor can the head say to the feet. "Well, I don't need you!"

All of you are Christ's body, and each one is a part of it.'

(1 Corinthians 12:12-17, 21, 27)

Gentiles: non-Jews

Classwork

B. Read Colossians 1:18 and Ephesians 4:15–16.
  1. What else does Paul say about the Church as the Body of Christ?
  2. Use all you have learned about the Church as the body of Christ to design an advertisement to encourage people to join the Church today.

C. Think of another image that would express Paul's message about the unity of Christ and the Church. Present your ideas in any form you choose.

Living community

My name is Harry. I was really surprised when my twin came home from church and said that Father Tom wanted everyone to bring a stone to church. 'What for?' I said.

'For the new altar,' said Hilary. 'Father Tom said everyone's stones are going to be part of the new altar. There'll be a glass side so that everyone can see them. It's a sign that we are God's building. The stones can't be more than five centimetres. I'm going to take the stone I got on the beach when we went to Llandudno. It's round and shiny and blue. I'll be able to see it through the glass.'

'I haven't got a stone,' I said.

'Well, you'll have to find one,' said Hilary. She can be so bossy.

The next time I went to church I had a look at the drawings of what the altar would look like. The title said 'We are the Living Stones of the Lord's House'. I still didn't have a stone to take. Grandad gave me the idea about what to do. 'Take your fossil,' he said, 'I bet it'll be the oldest stone there.'

'Stone Sunday' came. Father Tom blessed all the stones. They were all different sizes and different colours. Some were round and some looked quite sharp. I think mine was the only one with a fossil. Father Tom said the altar was a symbol of Jesus. That's why the priest kisses the altar at the beginning of Mass, to remember Jesus' love for everyone. The stones will remind us that Jesus makes us one family.

The Archbishop came to bless the new altar on Thursday. Afterwards there was a party at the convent.

People wrote about their stones in the newsletter.

> Five stones are from our family grave in County Limerick.
>
> It comes from Cumbria where my maternal family had its home.
>
> Found in Israel at the sea of Galilee.
>
> Brought from Trinidad when my Gran's mum came to England.
>
> Mine is a piece of the garden wall of our house.

From the prayers for the blessing of the altar:

Make this altar a sign of Christ…

Make it a table of joy…

Make it a place of communion and peace…

Make it a source of unity and friendship…

From the entrance hymn:

> Built of tears and cries and laughter,
> Prayers of faith and songs of grace,
> Let this house proclaim from floor to rafter:
> All are welcome, all are welcome, all are
> welcome in this place.
>
> Marty Haugen

Homework

Two images

All of you are Christ's body, and each one is a part of it. (1 Corinthians 12:27)

Come as living stones and let yourselves be used in building the spiritual temple where you will serve as holy priests to offer spiritual and acceptable sacrifices to God through Jesus Christ. (1 Peter 2:5)

Which image do you like best? Use it to prepare an outline for a Year 7 assembly.

Share your ideas with the class.

Divided body

For almost fifteen centuries the Christian community in England and Wales was one body. Then, for about 400 years, Christians persecuted each other because of their differences. Later on we will be learning about the causes of these divisions and the work being done for Christian unity. In this section of work we will be learning about some of the different Christian Churches.

Find out the names of Christian Churches in your neighbourhood.

You could use the Internet, the telephone directory, local maps and the library.

Use a local map, or create one of your own, to show the Christian churches in your neighbourhood. Or, add to the map you made in 1A (p.11).

Testing times ❓

1. Where in the Bible will you find information about the life of the early Christians?
2. What images of the Church have you learned about in this section of your work?
3. What does the altar in a church represent?
4. In your own words, explain how Christians are 'living stones'.
5. Name four different Christian Churches.

Key words

For your Fact File:

building

community

One Body

unity

Pressure point

'I love the community. It's just people that I can't stand.'

Words of faith

And we, though many, throughout the earth, we are one body in this one Lord.

John Foley, *One Bread, One Body*

What does this invite Christians to be and do?

3D Celebrating life

In all the world

These pictures show universal symbols: that means they have meaning for people everywhere. Choose six symbols. Choose words from the Wordstore that express the meaning of each of the symbols. You may use some words more than once. You may want to add words of your own.

Wordstore

life, power, death, food, precious, nourishment, strength, mysterious, clean, friendship, good, love, frightening, cooling, growth, community, celebration, heat, new life, energy, treasured, happiness, care, satisfaction, limitless, life-giving, healing, awesome

Think and talk

Share your findings. Listen to others.
How many of your word choices were the same? How many were very different?
What does this tell you about the power of symbols?
Divide the symbols into two groups: the natural world and human life.

Create a design using your symbol.

Check out what you know ☑

Work with a partner.

List these parts of the Mass in correct order: opening prayer, readings, homily, collection, gospel, offertory, welcome, intercessions, Eucharistic prayer, sign of peace, Our Father, communion, sending forth.

Check out your answers with the class.

The Great Sacrament

Symbols open our minds and imaginations to something great and often more mysterious than themselves. The bread and wine at the Eucharist are signs of the great mystery that the Church celebrates in this sacrament. The bread and wine become the Body and Blood of Jesus. Those who receive his Body and Blood become one body in him. The sacrament of the Eucharist is the living symbol of the communion with Jesus that is vital for Christian living. (Look back to IC p. 23.)

Let's look at the rites and symbols of the sacrament to see what it means. The pictures and words follow the order of the celebration. Look at each group carefully and decide what symbols are being used. Remember that actions are also symbolic. Decide who is acting, what happens and what is said. What do the actions and words tell you about God and the Church, the People of God? Use a missal or mass book as a source for your work.

Entry rite

The Church gathers as the People of God.

In the name of the Father and of the Son and of the Holy Spirit.

They acknowledge their need of God.

I confess…

They sing a song of praise:

Glory to God.

The priest prays in the name of the people.

Liturgy of the Word

The Good News is proclaimed.

This is the Word of the Lord
Thanks be to God
Alleluia
This is the gospel of the Lord
Praise to you, Lord Jesus Christ

The Church professes its faith:
the Creed.
The Church prays for the needs
of the world: bidding prayers.

Liturgy of the Eucharist

The Church offers to God the gifts of creation and prays that they will become the Body and Blood of Jesus to be spiritual food and drink for his people.

Blessed are you Lord…

By the mingling of this water and wine…

The priest invites everyone to pray that the bread and wine offered will become part of the *sacrifice* of Jesus.

sacrifice: an offering to God

The priest prays that the power of the Holy Spirit will transform the gifts of bread and wine so that they will become the Body and Blood of Christ.

Using the words of Jesus at the Last Supper, he consecrates the bread and wine:

This is my body…

This is my blood…

Do this in memory of me.

The Church professes its faith.

Christ has died…

The Church prays in communion with Jesus.

Through him, with him, in him…

Amen

Rite of Communion

The Church prays as one body with Christ:

Our Father.

The Church expresses oneness through the sign of peace.

Those who have been initiated through Baptism and the Eucharist receive Holy Communion.

The Body of Christ.

Amen.

Concluding rite: the sending forth

The Church is sent forth in the name of God.

May Almighty God bless you, the Father, the Son and the Holy Spirit.

Go in peace to love and serve the Lord.

Thanks be to God.

All Christian life is here

Look at the pictures and words again. Think back over your work in Year 7. What links can you make? For example, between the Entry Rite and your work on community in 1A; between the prayers for the offering of the gifts of bread and wine and your work on creation (3A).

Work in groups, then share your findings with the class.

Create a display to show these links. How will you show the Eucharist at the centre of the display? How will you show the links to your work? What samples of your work will you use?

Give your display a title.

Think and talk: the sacrament of living

The Eucharist is commonly called Mass. How does it get this name? What does it mean? (Look back to 1A p.13.)

What is the Church sent forth to do?

Think of different people who would be at a parish Mass on Sunday.

Think of how they would live in peace and love and serve the Lord during the rest of the week.

Is there anything to add to your display?

Classwork

Celebrating Eucharist

A. Create a table to show the main parts of the celebration of the sacrament of the Eucharist. Identify symbols, symbolic actions, words and what they mean. Fill in your table.

B. Choose two parts of the Mass and explain in more detail what happens and what they mean.

C. Think about why first communion is a special moment in the Christian journey. Write a letter of congratulations to someone who is going to make their First Holy Communion. Write a prayer they can use after communion.

Homework

Copymaster 16

The presence of Jesus

The Eucharist is the greatest celebration because the Church believes that Jesus is present in a unique way.

Words we use

The sacrament of the Eucharist has several other names:

The Lord's Supper
because Christians remember the Last Supper that Jesus shared with his friends before he died.

The Breaking of Bread
because at the Last Supper Jesus broke bread and gave it to his disciples. The next day he gave himself, body and blood, on the cross.

Memorial Sacrifice
because it is in obedience to Jesus' command 'Do this in memory of me' and makes present his sacrifice on the cross.

Eucharist
means 'Thanksgiving'. The Church gives thanks to God the Father with Jesus.

Holy Communion
because Jesus shares himself and unites the Church as 'one body'.

3D Celebrating life

3

Making connections

Thought stop

Look beyond the bread you eat:
see your Saviour and your Lord.
Look beyond the cup you drink:
see his love poured out as blood.

Source unknown

Key *words*

· ·

For your Fact File:

Eucharist
Mass
presence
communion
Offertory
Liturgy of the Word
Liturgy of the Eucharist

Words of faith

What do these actions tell us about Jesus'
life, death and resurrection: 'Take, bless,
break, and give'?

Testing times ?

1. List the five parts of the celebration of Mass.

2. What are the words of consecration?

3. Give five ways Jesus is present in this sacrament.

4. What are Catholics supposed to do when the Mass is ended?

5. Give two other names for the sacrament of the Eucharist.

Pressure point

'If Mass is meant to be a celebration, why does everyone always look so serious?'
Maria, aged 11.

Holy Communion Song

1 Jesus took a loaf of bread:
   When the blessing he had said,
   Broke and gave it to his friends:
   'Take this and eat.'

Chorus
   Take, Bless, Break and Give:
   That's what Jesus did.
   Take, Bless, Break and Give:
   That's what Jesus did.

2 Jesus took a wine-filled cup,
   Thanks to God he offered up,
   Gave the cup out to his friends:
   'Take this and drink.'

Ernest Sands